CW00672005

CAPTAINS AND KINGS

Published by Sapere Books.

24 Trafalgar Road, Ilkley, LS29 8HH

United Kingdom

saperebooks.com

Copyright © The Estate of John Winton, 1981.

First published by Bluejacket Books, 1981.

The Estate of John Winton has asserted its right to be identified as the author of this work.

All rights reserved.

No part of this publication may be reproduced, stored in any retrieval system, or transmitted, in any form, or by any means, electronic, mechanical, photocopying, recording, or otherwise, without the prior written permission of the publishers.

ISBN: 978-1-80055-755-0.

TABLE OF CONTENTS

WHY DO YOU WANT TO JOIN THE NAVY?

'Why do you want to join the Navy?' It is the question the Admiral Interview Board always asks every candidate at some stage of his interview. It seems an obvious, indeed an essential, question to put to all those who want to become naval officers and one would expect every candidate to have prepared and rehearsed his answer. Yet it is odd how many candidates appear absolutely flummoxed by it. It seems to be an impossible question to answer without appearing pompous, or conceited, or sycophantic, or self-satisfied, or downright soft in the head. It is not just a question of what to answer, but *how* to answer. Speak up fluently and confidently and the Board will sit back with pursed lips, thinking, *Smartypants*. Stutter and hesitate, grope for the right words, and the Board will think, *this lad is a little touched: here he is, taking examinations, coming up before interview boards, and he doesn't even know why he is doing it!*

If it is difficult for the ordinary young man, what must it be for members of the Royal Family? The Navy is a hard life, as those who join it soon discover. There are plenty of brickbats and precious few bouquets. Their Lordships must rank well up in the list of the most ungrateful and bloody-minded employers of all time. The rule is to give and not to count the cost, to toil and not to seek for rest, to labour and not to seek for any reward save that of knowing that if you do *not*, somebody will most probably court-martial you.

The Navy vastly enjoys Royal occasions. There is nothing the Service likes better than a visit to the fleet by Her Majesty, with the sun shining, the Royal Standard flying, the Queen grinning widely, and the Royal Marine Band giving a gusty rendering of 'You Must Have Been a Beautiful Baby'. But in *professional* matters, in commanding a ship, or winning wings for helicopter flying, the Navy subjects everybody, no matter who they are, to the same bleak, unforgiving, professional scrutiny.

Thus, one of King George V's captains criticised his 'sense of responsibility'. King Edward VIII, as Cadet Prince Edward, and King George VI, as Cadet Prince Albert, were both given a very hard time at Osborne and Dartmouth. Prince Philip failed the torpedo and anti-submarine part of his destroyer command examination. Prince Charles and Prince Andrew, who have both undergone helicopter flying courses, both know what an unrelenting, critical appraisal they have survived: trainee pilots and observers can be, and some have been, dismissed from their course the day before they were due to get their wings.

To the Royal Family, the Navy is of course like a family firm. A truly staggering number of them have served. King George V joined as Cadet Prince George of Wales in 1877. He was promoted Captain in January 1893, and became an Admiral of the Fleet on his accession in May 1910. His two sons, Edward and Albert, joined as Cadets in 1907 and 1909, and both became Admirals of the Fleet on their accessions, King Edward VIII on 21st January 1936 and George VI on his brother's Abdication, on 11th December 1936. Their younger brother Prince George joined as a Cadet in 1917. He became Duke of Kent in October 1934, and was a Rear Admiral when he was killed in an air crash in August 1942.

Of their cousins, on the Battenberg side, Prince Louis of Battenberg joined as a Cadet in 1868 and was an Admiral and First Sea Lord when anti-German feeling in the country forced him to resign in October 1914. He became an Admiral of the Fleet in August 1921. His eldest son, Prince George, later 2nd

Marquess of Milford Haven, joined as a Cadet in 1905 and was a Captain when he died in 1938. His younger brother, Prince Louis, joined as a Cadet in 1913, rose to be First Sea Lord, and was promoted Admiral of the Fleet in October 1956. His nephew, Prince Philip, joined as a Cadet in 1939, was promoted Commander in 1952, and Admiral of the Fleet in January 1953. The 3rd Marquess, David Milford Haven, joined as a Cadet in 1933, was made OBE in 1942 and won a DSC in 1943, and retired as a Lieutenant Commander in 1948. Prince Philip's eldest son Charles, joined as a Sub Lieutenant — the highest joining rank of any of his family — in 1971, and retired from active service, as a Commander, in 1976. His younger brother, Prince Andrew, joined as a Midshipman in 1979.

On the distaff side, the Duchess of Kent, Princess Marina, became Commandant of the W.R.N.S. on the outbreak of the Second World War. Her niece, Princess Anne, is the present Chief Commandant of the W.R.N.S. Her Majesty the Queen herself is, of course, Lord High Admiral and head of the Navy.

Paradoxically, the Royal Family have always felt a greater sense of freedom when they were in the confined space of a ship. Going on board was one of their very few escape routes from what they themselves call the Royal 'cage'. There can be no doubt that the greatest service the Royal Yacht *Britannia* and her ship's company provide for the Queen and her family is privacy. King George VI, despite the strained look on his face in many of his photographs, never felt more at ease and at peace with himself and the world than when he visited one of his warships. One of the most carefree and pleasant interludes in the Queen's life was her stay in Malta, as Princess Elizabeth: she was a 'naval wife', living in a rented house, with a husband who was 'Jimmy' of a destroyer in the local flotilla. For a brief charmed period, the rigid grip of the Royal regime relaxed.

When the Prince of Wales went to sea in *Bronington*, he firmly left his private detective behind on the jetty. Credit, blame, responsibility, were then his alone, while he was in command.

The Royal Family have always looked on the Navy as excellent training for their responsibilities in life. When Prince George, the future King George V, had misgivings about his own capabilities after his brother's death, Prince Louis of Battenberg assured him that there was 'no more fitting preparation for a King than to have been trained in the Navy'. Lord Louis Mountbatten repeated the same advice, in the same words, to George VI when he was wracked with self-doubts at the time of the Abdication.

But above all, the Navy accords with what the Royal Family see as their duty to be of service. This duty has their highest priority. When Princess Elizabeth broadcast from South Africa on her 21st birthday, she began: 'I declare before you all that my whole life, whether it be long or short, shall be devoted to your service...' Her Majesty used the same words, in the same spirit, at her Jubilee in 1977.

The same belief was expressed, years before, by her father. Midshipman HRH Prince Albert was watch-keeping at his action station in the forrard turret of the dreadnought HMS *Collingwood* in the North Sea. It was very cold and very rough, and everybody was miserable; waves were flinging themselves over the turret and the whole Grand Fleet was tired of waiting for the Germans to come out. The gunlayer of the turret, Petty Officer James Moffatt, said to the Prince: 'I don't understand why you stick to this business, Prince Albert. I'd sooner be off than sitting here wet and freezing.

'He looked at me and smiled: I shall never forget his answer. "You are a freer man than I am, Moffatt. If you were allowed to go you could leave at any time. But if they said to me 'Go' I should be bound to stay." 'But why? What keeps you,' I persisted. "Public opinion keeps me here," he replied quietly. That day in the sea-beaten turret I learnt from Prince Albert that it is people like myself, the poor people of this world, who are freest of all. They do not always realise it, but it is a fact.'

KING GEORGE V

There is a saying that it is always the fool of the family who joins the Navy. Prince George Frederick Ernest Albert, known to the family as 'Georgie', joined the Navy with his elder brother, Prince Albert Victor, known as 'Eddy'. If anything, it was Eddy who was the fool of the family. The boy's tutor, Reverend John Neale Dalton, seemed permanently pessimistic about Prince Albert Victor's mental capacity and application. He said that Prince Albert Victor needed 'the stimulus of Prince George's company to induce him to work at all...' If Prince George was to join the Navy, then Prince Albert Victor should go with him. 'Difficult as the education of Prince Albert Victor is now, it would be doubly or trebly so if Prince George were to leave him. Prince George's lively presence is his mainstay and chief incentive to exertion...'

In fact, Mr Dalton thought Prince Albert Victor unsuitable for a naval career. However, he thought the life in the old wooden-wall training ship *Britannia*, lying in the Dart, would 'improve His Royal Highness's moral, mental and physical development'. Such sentiments would have greatly surprised many of the cadets actually in *Britannia* but, Mr Dalton went on, it would provide him with 'physical and mental tone', and help him develop 'those habits of promptitude and method, of manliness and self-reliance, in which he is now somewhat deficient'.

Queen Victoria did not agree at first. She would have preferred the boys to go somewhere like Wellington College, living in some house in the vicinity, so that they could have the public school life but 'with none of its resultant dangers'.

Eventually she did agree. But she said that 'Eddy is not to go aloft'.

The Queen thought the Navy 'a very rough sort of life' and 'the very thing *not* calculated to make a refined and amiable Prince who in after years (if God spares him) is to ascend the throne...' It was different for Georgie. A rough sort of life did not matter if one was not the heir to the throne. Georgie passed into *Britannia* in the summer of 1877 and joined in July.

The two Princes had their own cabin, and Mr Dalton was there to look after them, but otherwise they shared the usual life of *Britannia*: hard physical effort, cold salt-water baths, and strict discipline. There were periodic bouts of bullying. Cadets were no respecters of Royal persons. There was much to be said in favour of punching a Royal nose and tapping the Royal claret. 'It never did me any good to be a Prince, I can tell you,' said Prince George in later years, 'and many was the time I wished I hadn't been. It was a pretty tough place and, so far from making any allowances for our disadvantages, the other boys made a point of taking it out of us on the grounds that they'd never be able to do it later on.'

'There was a lot of fighting among the cadets and the rule was that if challenged you had to accept. So they used to make me go up and challenge the bigger boys — I was awfully small then — and I'd get a hiding time and again. But one day I was landed a blow on the nose which made my nose bleed badly. It was the best blow I ever took for the Doctor forbade my fighting any more.'

While Prince Albert Victor seemed constitutionally lethargic, Prince George thrived and did well in *Britannia*, in spite of his various trials. He was academically bright, and had good physical and mental co-ordination. His only real problem was the constant persecution. There was 'a sort of tuckshop on land, up the steep hill; only we weren't allowed to bring any eatables into the ship, and they used to search you as you came aboard. Well, the big boys used to fag me to bring them back a whole lot of stuff — and I was always found out and got into trouble in addition to having the stuff confiscated. And the worst of it was, it was always *my* money; they never paid me back — I suppose they thought there was plenty more where that came from, but in point of fact we were only given a shilling a week pocket money, so it meant a lot to me, I can tell you.'

The Princes' parents, the Prince and Princess of Wales, visited *Britannia* in the summer of 1878, to distribute the prizes. Prince George passed out of *Britannia* quite creditably in July the following year. Nothing was said about Prince Albert Victor.

After *Britannia*, George was supposed to go on a long cruise round the world, while Albert Victor went to a public school. But Mr Dalton advised that the boys be kept together; by himself, Albert Victor would appear all the more backward. So both boys embarked in the 4,000-ton corvette HMS *Bacchante* (Captain Lord Charles Scott) which left Spithead for Gibraltar on 17th September 1879. There were nine midshipmen on board, and four other cadets — George Hardinge, Rosslyn Wemyss, Hillyard and Osborne — of the Princes' *Britannia* term. Mr Dalton complained of the Senior Midshipman Mr E. L. Munro, that his 'almost feminine ways and silly deference to them (the Princes) induced them to take liberties with him which they should not'. Mr Munro was removed after the first cruise, on the grounds of ill health.

In all, the Princes did three cruises: the first, from September 1879 to May 1880, to the Mediterranean and the West Indies; the second, from July to August 1880, to Bantry Bay and Vigo;

and the third, from September 1880 to August 1882, with Lord Clanwilliam's Detached Squadron, went right round the world, to the West Indies, South America, the Cape, Australia, Fiji, Japan, Hong Kong, Singapore, Colombo, Suez and home through the Mediterranean. It was excellent sea-going experience, although there had been earlier doubts about *Bacchante's* seaworthiness which, off Australia in May 1881, seemed well-founded. The ship's rudder was damaged in a storm and for a time it was thought that *Bacchante* had been lost, with every soul on board.

Once again. Prince George shone, compared with his elder brother. In *Britannia* he had told the seamanship instructors not to bother about his brother, who was not going to sea, but to concentrate upon him instead. In *Bacchante*, he passed examinations for the rank of midshipman and generally did well. Prince Albert Victor did not, 'in spite of the kindly encouragement,' said Mr Dalton, 'given him to work by his younger brother and by other of his messmates'.

The difference between the two brothers was well, if tactfully, put by Lord Napier, Governor of Gibraltar. 'The youngest,' he said, in November 1879, 'is the most lively and popular, but I think the eldest is better suited to his situation — he is shy and not demonstrative, but he does the right things as a young gentleman in a quiet way.'

Hillyard was Prince George's messmate for some five years, and came to know him well. 'The companionship in one of Her Majesty's gunrooms in those days was of necessity a very close and intimate one. Weeks and weeks at sea, sometimes very monotonous weeks, living on food that was more than monotonous, and also exceedingly nasty. Mostly salt pork and ship's biscuits. Remember there were no comforts in those days. No such things as electrical freezing plant. So fresh vegetables, fruit and fresh provisions lasted a very, very short time after leaving harbour. Also, one got rather bored at always seeing the same old faces round the same old table, and tempers at times were apt to get a little frayed and irritable. Yet in all those years I never remember Prince George losing his temper. I certainly never had even a cross word with him. Unselfish, kindly, good-tempered, he was an ideal shipmate.'

After *Bacchante*, the two Princes were sent to Lausanne to learn French. When they came back, Eddy's short naval career was over. But George was appointed Midshipman in the corvette HMS *Canada* (Captain Francis Durrant) on the North American and West Indies Station. His family were determined George was not to receive special treatment. His uncle, Vice Admiral HRH the Duke of Edinburgh, Queen Victoria's second son, had himself been promoted Captain at the age of 22 and ever afterwards felt that this was something to be lived down in the eyes of the Navy. Durrant was told by the Queen and by the Prince of Wales that Prince George was to be treated like everybody else, so he lived in the gunroom, slept in a hammock, kept watches and ran a boat like all other midshipmen.

Prince George was promoted Acting Sub Lieutenant in June 1884 and came home for courses in July. He went to the Royal Naval College, Greenwich, where he worked hard and did well. One of his instructors, Mr. J. L. Robinson, praised his 'habits of sound and honest work'. He said he only wished that 'his example in these important respects and his good sense were followed by all young officers.' The President reported that Prince George had 'passed a very satisfactory examination'.

In March 1885, Prince George went to *Excellent* for a gunnery course. That summer Queen Victoria wrote to him to 'Avoid the many evil temptations wh. beset *all* young men and especially Princes. Beware of flatterers, too great love of amusement, of *races* & betting & playing high'.

The Queen had no need to worry. Prince George got a first class pass in gunnery, in torpedoes and in seamanship; he missed a first in pilotage by a few marks; the story was that one of his examiners, an old salt-horse sailor, 'didn't think it would do to let him fancy he knew all about it'. Prince George was promoted Lieutenant on 8th October 1885. Captain John Fisher, commanding *Excellent*, wrote to Queen Victoria: 'He has with great tact and good judgement, and quite of his own accord, declined many invitations, kindly meant to give him pleasure, but which would have taken him from his work besides bringing him more prominently into public notice than your Majesty might have thought desirable under the circumstances.' The First Lord of the Admiralty, Lord George Hamilton, sent the exam results to the Prince of Wales saying that 'the capacity which Prince George has shown is unusual'. The Prince of Wales was delighted. '… No favouritism in your case!' he told his son.

There is no doubt that the Prince was becoming a most able officer. He had tended to be headstrong and excitable ('Right Royal Pickle' was one of the family's nicknames for him in infancy). Durrant had reported that 'his sense of responsibility is in need of encouragement'. But his formative years in the Navy had steadied and strengthened him. It was no wonder that he came to think the Navy the best of all possible training schools for his own sons.

This promising start might have been spoiled when he went to the Mediterranean in 1886, where he served in the ironclads *Thunderer*, *Dreadnought* and *Alexandra*. The Med. was not only the strategic but the social centre of the Navy in those days. His uncle 'Affie', the Duke of Edinburgh was C-in-C. George went to balls, to picnics, and swimming parties. He played polo on his two ponies 'Real Jam' and 'Blackthorn'. He grew a beard. He went to Athens to see his uncle the King of the Hellenes and Queen Olga who called him 'my little sunbeam'. Fortunately, the little sunbeam had a steadying influence in Captain Henry Stephenson, in *Thunderer*, who was his father's great friend and came in time to be guide, philosopher and friend to Prince George himself.

In June 1887, Prince George came home on leave to attend Queen Victoria's Golden Jubilee. In April 1889 he left the Mediterranean Station and went to do his lieutenant's courses in gunnery at *Excellent* and torpedoes at *Vernon*. After courses he was appointed to the cruiser HMS *Northumberland* as a watch-keeping Lieutenant. Then he had a bit of luck. On 18th July he commissioned Torpedo Boat No. 79, his first independent command.

The 75-ton TB 79 was launched in 1886, was 125 feet long, 13 feet wide and drew 5 feet six inches. She could do 22½ knots, had a ship's company of 15; the only other officer was the Gunner, with whom Prince George 'shared his tiny cabin and his box of sardines'. TB 79 was one of the 109 warships present on 6th August for the Spithead Review in honour of Prince George's cousin, William II of Germany, who had been made Honorary Admiral of the Fleet four days earlier.

After the Review, TB 79 steamed up the coast of Ireland for exercises. She was a 'wet' boat. She rolled inordinately and tried always to steam through a wave instead of over it. The weather was bad and Prince George suffered from seasickness. 'Rather seedy' was a frequent phrase in his letters. In one exercise, to defend Lough Swilly, TB 79 and two others were set to sea after dark to scout for the enemy.

Returning to harbour, after a miserable night, TB 41 broke down at daylight and had to anchor close to a lee shore. After one unsuccessful attempt, Prince George got a hemp hawser aboard 41 and towed her safely off. It was a neat piece of seamanship in very rough weather, with waves breaking over 79's upper deck. 'It has been a most damnable day,' he wrote in his diary. 'Very tired. Up all night. Was terribly seasick.' 'I can tell you I was pleased to get in,' he wrote to Stephenson, 'as we certainly have had a very rough time of it all, the manoeuvres and shocking bad weather, but beyond being seasick several times, I never felt better in my life...'

Prince George was appointed to the Royal Yacht *Osborne* as an additional lieutenant. He had only been on board a few days when he was put out to discover from Hardinge his old shipmate, still in *Northumberland*, that the position had never been clarified and they were still one lieutenant short. Prince George was always very sensitive to any inference that his was a special case. 'These sort of mistakes only make me very unpopular in the Service...' he wrote to Stephenson, asking him to sort the matter out.

Osborne went to Athens and then to Egypt in November 1889. There was 'a gale in our teeth all the way to Port Said,' Prince George wrote, 'and I was naturally horribly seasick...' His sickness was a real affliction for him. In May 1890 he commissioned the gunboat *Thrush* at Chatham. Stephenson sailed with him as a passenger as far as Dover. *Thrush* sailed on 1st June for the North American Station, towing a gunboat behind her, and reached it via Ferrol, Gibraltar and Bermuda. Off Ferrol, 'we knocked about a good deal all night and needless to say I was seasick...'

Thrush returned to England in August 1891. She received a good inspection report and paid off on 23rd August. Prince

George was promoted to Commander the next day. He had now emerged as a thoroughly competent naval officer. Although it would never have been possible for him to lead an entirely normal naval life — he would always have been liable to be called away on 'Royal business' — he would have become an admiral in due course, on merit. He had a group of close friends in the Navy, mostly term-mates, such as 'Rosy' Wemyss, Charles Cust, George Hillyard and Charles Dormer.

But, in January 1892, Prince George's personal and professional life changed completely. In December 1891, Prince Eddy had become engaged to marry Princess Mary of Teck. Prince George was just recovering from an attack of typhoid fever and was convalescing at Marlborough House. He was able to go to Sandringham by the end of December but, on 7th January, Eddy fell ill with influenza. Pneumonia set in on 13th, and by 9.35 on the morning of the next day he was dead.

The Duke of York, as the Prince became on 24th May 1892, was now second in line to the throne and his active naval career was over. He did commission the cruiser *Melampus* for a few weeks' manoeuvres in the summer of 1892. Charles Cust was one of her officers and Hugh Evan-Thomas, who had been a midshipman in *Bacchante*, was First Lieutenant. There was also a 'capital French cook' on board.

The Duke was promoted Captain on 2nd January 1893 and his very last sea command was the cruiser *Crescent*, which he commissioned for about eight weeks' exercises in the summer of 1898; the sea-time also qualified him for the rank of Rear Admiral to which he was promoted on 1st January 1901.

George not only took Eddy's place in the succession but also his fiancée. He was engaged to Mary of Teck on 4th May 1893. They were married in the Chapel Royal, St. James's on 6th July.

Although he had left the Navy for all practical purposes, the Duke recognised the Navy's influence on him. 'I think I am entitled,' he told the cadets of the training ship *Conway*, at their prizegiving in July 1899, 'from a personal experience of twenty years at sea, to impress on you three qualities... truthfulness, obedience and zeal. Truthfulness will give those placed under you confidence in you, and obedience will give those placed over you confidence in you, and although I have mentioned zeal last, it is by no means the least important, for without zeal no sailor can be worth his salt...' Finally, the Duke did his own duty by asking for an extra week's holiday for the cadets.

The Duke of York became Duke of Cornwall automatically when his father became the reigning monarch in January 1901. It was as Duke of Cornwall and York that he sailed with his Duchess in the liner *Ophir* ('Rosy' Wemyss was Commander) from Portsmouth on 16th March 1901, for an Empire Tour. When *Ophir* returned on 1st November, the Duke had visited Gibraltar, Aden, Ceylon, Singapore, Australia, New Zealand, Mauritius, Cape Town, Canada and Newfoundland. He and his Duchess had travelled 45,000 miles, 33,000 by sea and 12,000 by land, laid 21 foundation stones, received 544 addresses, presented 4,329 medals and shaken hands with 24,855 people at official receptions alone. The Duke's reward was to be created Prince of Wales on 9th November 1901 — a title his father had borne for nearly sixty years.

The Prince of Wales was in a unique position as regards the Navy. He was as widely respected in the Service as he was well-known. Everybody knew he had joined as a lad in *Britannia* and had survived the rough and tumble of a midshipman's life. He had served at sea, if not quite for the twenty years he had told the *Conways*, then certainly for sixteen years, with intermittent service later. He had many long-standing friends in the Navy and a deep knowledge of the Service.

The great reforms in the Navy pressed forward by Admiral Fisher would have been much easier to accomplish if they had been whole-heartedly supported by the Prince of Wales. But, unfortunately, the Prince often chose the reactionary way. He came to oppose some of Fisher's reforms. He often did not agree with Fisher's choice of officers for the higher posts, almost always preferring somebody more conservative, more of a 'courtier' and less of a reformer. It almost seems that the Prince of Wales secretly hankered for the Navy to stay as it had been when he was a young man.

But first, he approved of Fisher's plans to change officers' training by having everybody, whatever their eventual specialisation, start off together. 'I call it a grand scheme and wish it every success,' he wrote to Fisher in November 1902. 'No doubt it will be severely criticised, especially by the *old ones*, who are too conservative for our modern days.' He approved of lowering the entry age back to what it was in his day, between 12 and 13 years old. 'You can't get them too young. I am certain the Navy will greatly benefit by having your Engineer and Marine officers drawn from the same class as your Executive officers. And it must abolish the present Engineers' complaints'. (Ironically, it was the Engineer and Marine officers who eventually were *not* fully integrated into the Fisher scheme.)

Fisher was greatly encouraged. 'I've been having a brisk correspondence with the Prince of Wales,' he told his son Cecil in April 1903. 'He is most cordial and friendly and has helped me immensely...' After the Royal Academy dinner in May, Fisher said the Prince 'was very delighted and cheered me like anything, but I think he's rather partial to me.'

The Prince saw 'an enormous future for submarines' and went down in A1 with Fisher at Portsmouth in March 1904. The Princess of Wales said 'I shall be very disappointed if George doesn't come up again'. They all laughed at the time but a week later Fisher was writing to the Prince with details of A1's loss — rammed and sunk by the liner *Berwick Castle* off the Isle of Wight.

Fisher brought home dozens of old, slow and small warships from their foreign stations and scrapped them, concentrating the Navy's main force in the Channel and the North Sea. The Prince disapproved. 'If you are going to remove the squadron in the Pacific because the ships are obsolete, you ought to send some new ones to take their place, at least that is my opinion,' he told Fisher. There spoke the old Navy, accustomed to 'showing the flag' on a dozen stations abroad.

In April 1906, Captain Reginald Bacon wrote to Fisher from HMS *Irresistible*, off Corfu, to tell him that the Prince of Wales had just arrived and 'seized on me at once, and was full of the opposition he had heard of in some quarters of the Navy to the new schemes of reform and that the Navy was becoming full of cliques, which was bad...' Bacon, who was Fisher's man, believed the Prince 'evidently has been badly "got at" by the opposition...' Bacon told the Prince the Navy was 'ultra-conservative and hated reforms'. The Prince wondered whether 'somehow the scheme might have been introduced with less friction'.

However, Fisher and the Prince of Wales had a friendly lunch together in October which reassured Fisher. As late as February 1908 Fisher still thought of the King and the Prince of Wales as 'both solid friends.' In July the Prince went to Canada in the new dreadnought battlecruiser *Indomitable*. He was delighted with her strength and speed — especially her speed; on passage home she steamed 2,880 miles in five days 18 hours 40 minutes — an average of nearly 21 knots.

The Great Feud between Fisher and Admiral Lord Charles Beresford split the Navy's officer *corps* in two. One was either a Fisherite, a denizen of the 'Fish Pond', or a Beresfordian, and never the twain shall meet. Despite pleas and counterpleas from his former naval colleagues, the Prince stayed publicly and outwardly neutral. In private he strongly deprecated (and he was an outspoken man when roused) this internal warfare in the Service. It was not good for the country and not good for the Navy.

Bacon had continued to write his letters to Fisher. They were strictly private but Fisher, looking for ammunition against Beresford, had them printed. This action seemed to turn the Prince of Wales against Fisher. At Newmarket in October 1909, the Prince met Beresford and became 'quite violent' about Fisher. Beresford himself said 'I could have said nothing stronger.' Knollys, the Prince's Secretary, said the Prince 'takes up far too violent and partizan tone both about 'Jackie' and the Admiralty...'

Fisher soon became aware of this change and it affected his own attitude towards the Prince, when he became King, and towards the monarchy in general. He began to liken King George V to Rehoboam (1.Kings 12.v.8) who 'forsook the counsel of the old men, which they had given him, and consulted with the young men that were grown up with him'. In 1911, over the appointment of an Elder Brother of Trinity House, the King scratched out one name and put in his own nominee: this 'episode', Fisher said bitterly, 'was about the dirtiest underhand trick ever played by King George...' Fisher was quite taken aback a few months later when the King sent him a haunch of venison. 'I thought I was off the list!' he said.

One of King George V's first acts on acceding to the throne was to send a message to the Navy, expressing his gratitude for its faithful and distinguished services to his beloved father. 'Educated and trained in that profession which I love so dearly,' he said, on 10th May 1910, 'retirement from active duty has in no sense diminished my feelings of affection for it.'

The King was not just affectionate, but personally and intensely interested in all aspects of the Navy. He had several clashes with Winston Churchill who became First Lord of the Admiralty in 1911. The King was not sure he trusted Churchill and accepted his appointment only with reluctance. In November 1911, the two men had a serious dispute over ships' names.

Warships' names were close to the King's heart. By hallowed tradition, the King chose the names. They were, after all, His Majesty's own ships. When Churchill put forward four names, *Africa*, *Liberty*, *Assiduous* and *Oliver Cromwell*, for a new class of battleship, the King would only accept *Africa*.

In March 1912, the King proposed *Delhi*, *Wellington* and *Marlborough*. Churchill accepted *Marlborough*, persuaded the King to have *Iron Duke* instead of *Wellington*, but was against *Delhi*, feeling it should be a cruiser's name. The King, according to Lord Stamfordham's letter to Churchill, 'was sorry that he does not like giving up the *Delhi*. In fact he held strongly to it as an appropriate name for one of the other battleships. It would suitably mark the year in which the capital of India was changed to Delhi'. So Churchill agreed.

In October 1912, Churchill submitted four more names for the battleship class of 1912–13: *King Richard the First*, *King Henry the Fifth*, *Queen Elizabeth*, and, once again, *Oliver Cromwell*. This was remarkably obtuse of Churchill, but ships' names seemed to find him at his most obstinate. He said he had consulted the

Prime Minister about *Oliver Cromwell* and he agreed with the view 'that the almost unequalled services which the Lord Protector rendered to the British Navy should find recognition in Your Majesty's Fleet'.

But the King had already turned *Oliver Cromwell* down once and he was, if it were possible, even more adamant now. He had the submission returned as 'he feels sure there must be some mistake in the name of *Oliver Cromwell* being suggested...'

Churchill should have let it go at that. But he did not. He persisted and pointed out that Cromwell was one of the founders of the Navy. Very few men had done more for the Navy than Oliver Cromwell. In a letter of 1st November 1912 Churchill summoned all his considerable powers of rhetoric: '... nothing in history will justify the view that the adoption of such a name would constitute any reflection, however vague, upon His Majesty's Royal House... His Majesty is the heir of all the glories of the nation... I am satisfied that the name will be extremely well received...'

But it was no use. The King was totally unmoved. The Second Sea Lord, Prince Louis of Battenberg, told Churchill that 'from all times the Sovereign's decisions as to the names for H.M. Ships has been accepted as final by all First Lords'. But Churchill returned to the charge, quoting eminent historians and saying that 'it certainly seems right that we should give to a battleship a name that never failed to make the enemies of England tremble.' Lord Stamfordham replied that nothing had changed the King's opinion, and he asked for another name. Churchill submitted *Valiant*, which was accepted.

Even now, Churchill did not give up. A year later he proposed *Pitt* and *Ark Royal*. But the King saw 'nothing in the records of former vessels to render a revival of these names essential'. Rear Admiral de Chair, the Naval Secretary, said that the King had *actually* said 'I do not wish any ship in my Navy to bear the name of a man who was responsible for the beheading of the reigning sovereign, and as to a ship carrying the name of Pitt, I know enough of the lower deck to realise that the bluejackets would alter it to another word of four letters'. When Churchill heard that, he said 'I think that unworthy of the royal mind.' But he had to give in.

But the King was never difficult or obstructive just for the sake of it. When there was a good case for economics in the upkeep of the Royal Yacht *Victoria and Albert*, for example, he readily agreed.

On 9th and 10th May 1912, King George V visited the fleet at Weymouth. The King, Prince Albert, and Mr Balfour all went for a three mile trip in the submarine D.4, commanded by Lieutenant Martin Nasmith. There were two innovations, aircraft flying over the sea looking for submarines, and the dropping of explosive bombs from the air. According to the Annual Register, 'the satisfactory state of the First British line of defence … was impressed on the public.'

The next large Royal Fleet Review was at the outbreak of war, on 17th and 18th July 1914. A trial mobilisation had begun on 15th July of the three fleets: the First Fleet, which was always fully manned and in full commission; the Second Fleet, which had been partly manned and was brought up to full complement; and the Third Fleet, normally wholly in reserve but brought out of reserve and specially commissioned. There was no legal authority at that time to compel men on the reserve to join, but some 20,000 presented themselves voluntarily at naval depots. The Review included 57 capital ships and, in Churchill's words, was 'incomparably the greatest assemblage of naval power ever witnessed in the history of the world.'

The King enthusiastically visited and inspected ships of every class and kind, after which the fleet put to sea for exercises. Every ship manned the side and gave three hearty cheers for His Majesty as she passed the Royal Yacht, anchored and flying the Royal Standard off the Nab, while seaplanes and aircraft flew overhead. At 15 knots it took almost six hours for every ship there to steam past.

When war was declared, the King sent a message to Sir John Jellicoe: 'At this grave moment in our national history, I send to you and through you to the officers and men of the fleet of which you have assumed command, the assurance of my confidence that under your direction they will revive and renew the old glories of the Royal Navy, and prove once again the sure shield of Britain and of her Empire in the hour of trial'. The message was very well received: 'I for one believe he writes his messages to the Navy himself,' said Lieutenant Stephen King-Hall, in the cruiser *Southampton*.

The signal covered a personal tragedy which the King tried to mitigate. The commander of the First Fleet, to be known as the Grand Fleet, was Admiral Sir George Callaghan, who had trained his ships for this hour and who had expected to command them in battle. But Churchill replaced Callaghan with his second-in-command, Jellicoe.

It was a brave, wise and proper decision. But it was an absolutely shattering emotional blow to Callaghan. He had loved and served the Navy, man and boy. At the very time when all his hopes and hard work were to be put to the test, he was removed and replaced by his junior. It was also a very painful experience for the officers of the fleet, not least for Jellicoe, who was the most loyal of men.

Callaghan's bitter disappointment was partly assuaged by the many letters he received, from Jellicoe amongst others. Nothing would ever ease the blow to his pride but still, as he wrote to Jellicoe in his reply, 'it was a hard time, but we will forget it as we doubtless will both have many more shocks before it is over. The King was most kind and did a great deal to put me right with myself...' So the King played an unobtrusive but important part in restoring Sir George's morale.

It was not long before the King was involved in another personal tragedy, this time concerning the First Sea Lord, Prince Louis of Battenberg. He had joined the Navy in October 1868 and risen to the height of his profession through merit. He was hard-working, intelligent, far-sighted, loyal and lovable, although he could never quite stand up to Churchill in Board debate, and perhaps his brilliant character lacked that ultimate steel stiffening.

He was born a German and although he had become naturalised there had been rumblings and whisperings of slander over his German birth and relations ever since 1911, when the Agadir crisis arose from an episode of clumsy German gunboat diplomacy. When war broke out, the British general public made an unattractive spectacle of itself in one of its fits of extreme xenophobia, and particularly Teutophobia. Dachshunds were chivvied and stoned in the street. Pork butchers had their windows broken. Anything German by name or association was liable to be jostled and insulted.

For Prince Louis, the slanders went deeper and closer. There was even gossip in Service clubs in St James that he was a German spy, or knew of German spies. It was a fantastic proposition. There never was a more loyal officer. Several of his relations had already given their lives for the Allies: his brother Prince Henry was killed in West Africa, his nephew Prince Maurice had been killed during the retreat from Mons. His two sons, George and Louis, were both serving in the Navy — Louis, the younger, the future First Sea Lord, having just gone to Osborne as a cadet.

The slanders so preyed on Prince Louis' mind that, rightly or wrongly, he decided that the country's Navy could not be directed in a war against Germany by a man with such overt German connections. On 28th October 1914 he sent a sad little letter to Churchill — 'I have lately been driven to the painful conclusion that at this juncture my birth and parentage have the effect of impairing in some respects my usefulness on the Board of Admiralty. In these circumstances I feel it to be my duty, as a loyal subject of His Majesty, to resign the office of First Sea Lord, hoping thereby to facilitate the task of the administration of the great Service, to which I have devoted my life, and to ease the burden laid on H.M. Ministers'.

Possibly if somebody had taken Prince Louis aside and impressed strongly enough on him that he should stay, he might have done. But Churchill did not try. He replied next day 'In all the circumstances you are right in your decision'. So, one of the most brilliant Royal naval careers of all came to an end, in an atmosphere of cat-calling and xenophobic jeering. Prince Louis, later the First Marquess of Milford Haven, was left to his collection of medals, and his memories.

That day of 29th October was 'most worrying and trying' for the King. To his utter consternation he found that Battenberg was to be replaced by Fisher, on whom he had not set eyes for at least six years. When Churchill came to tell him, the King did all he could to prevent the appointment. He told Churchill Fisher 'was not trusted by the Navy and they had no confidence in him personally.' The King thought it a great mistake. But in the end he had to give in 'with great reluctance…'

The King even appealed to the Prime Minister. But Mr Asquith insisted. So the King asked that his 'misgivings' be recorded, and signed the appointment. When Asquith had gone, the King saw 'poor Louis, very painful interview, he quite broke down.' The King made him a Privy Councillor to show the confidence he had in him, 'which pleased him'.

The King told Asquith he hoped his 'fears may prove groundless'. Next day, 30th October, he received Fisher. 'He is now 74. He seems as young as ever,' said the King enigmatically. 'I only trust he will do well at the Admiralty'.

The King was actually wrong in saying the Navy did not trust Fisher. Beatty said 'I think he is the best they could have done' although Beatty did wish that 'he was ten years younger'.

Fisher was under no illusions about the King's opinion of him. He himself now regarded the King as an opponent. In May 1914 he wrote to Jellicoe complaining that 'the King and his pimps are starting another crusade to revert to the old lines' (by obstructing parts of the new training scheme for officers — the status of engineer officers in particular, was proving an indigestible lump for the King and many officers of the old school to swallow).

Only four days before he became First Sea Lord, Fisher had been telling George Lambert, the Civil Lord of the Admiralty, that he was going abroad because 'I don't see any use my being in England with the dead set at me by the King, and the Prime Minister "kowtowing" to him!' And when ruminating over the setbacks of the past he told Lambert 'the person chiefly responsible is the present King, who blazed away at my policy to all and every person who came near him!' Fisher could be witheringly sarcastic. 'Just off to see the King,' he told Beatty, in December 1914, 'who wants me urgently, he says. Probably Prince Albert has got stomach ache!'

Yet, although Fisher set about his task with almost all his old fire and energy, the King was right. He proved he knew more about the Navy than his politicians and his advisers. In May 1915, Fisher suddenly resigned. The ostensible reason was the question of the scale of naval reinforcements for the expedition to the Dardanelles. But the real reason was the long period of disagreement and muscle-testing with Churchill. The two strong-minded and strong-willed characters simply could not get on.

Fisher just left, leaving everybody puzzled by his disappearance. He wrote to the King listing the 593 vessels including 24 airships laid down since he had taken over on 30th October. The King thanked him for his 'very important letter'. But at the same time the King was disgusted by the resignation, which he thought was 'bound to have a deplorable, if not disastrous, effect upon the public, not only at home, but abroad'. Asquith and the Sea Lords were also shocked.

Fisher's resignation also helped to pull down Churchill. The King favoured Balfour as First Lord because he thought Churchill had 'become impossible'. He advised that Fisher's resignation should be accepted quickly, or it might seem that Balfour's first act was to get rid of Fisher. Churchill left the Admiralty on 21st May 1915.

The King remained very angry at what he saw as Fisher's desertion of his post. Fisher was not mentioned in the King's speech after the Armistice. The King told a house party at Balmoral in 1921 that if he had been in London when Fisher was finally found he would have told him that he ought to have been hanged at the yardarm for desertion of his post in the face of the enemy. The King thought it 'really was most scandalous behaviour which ought to have been punished with dismissal from the Service with degradation'. An eyewitness said that 'the King got so angry that he became quite red in the face at the recollection of Fisher's actions'.

From the war's first day, the King made it his business literally to show himself to his people and his armed forces. He went over to see the army in France and Belgium on seven occasions, the first being in November 1914. Sometimes with Queen Mary, but often alone, he visited over 300 naval and military units and the same number of factories engaged on war-work.

The King's tours were not only a tremendous physical strain but often an emotional and psychological ordeal. The horrific casualty lists which soon filled whole pages several columns wide in *The Times* began to translate themselves into line after line of sickbeds, full of the shell-shocked, the men with horrible blast and shrapnel wounds, the amputees and the mentally deranged. Indefatigably, the King toured some 400 hospitals, tirelessly walking through ward after ward, looking into sightless eyes, shaking the stumps of amputated limbs, speaking encouragingly to men who in their privately crazed worlds of pain and madness hardly knew who was addressing them.

Perhaps the most staggering statistic was the number of decorations and awards the King personally conferred, shaking the hand of recipients: 58,000, or nearly 40 for every day the war lasted. He knew how much an Investiture meant to the man or woman concerned. On 28th October 1915, when he was in France inspecting the 1st Wing, Royal Flying Corps, his mare was frightened by the men's cheering, reared up, slipped, and fell back on top of the King, fracturing his pelvis in two places.

The King was very badly injured and in great pain. It was four weeks before he could even hobble about on two sticks. Yet he invested Lance Sergeant Oliver Brooks of the Coldstream Guards with his Victoria Cross, from his sickbed in the ambulance train taking him to Boulogne.

Although the country was engaged in a desperate war, the King never forgot why the war was being fought. There were certain standards to be kept up, even towards the enemy — *particularly* towards the enemy. In April 1915 the King discovered that captured U-boat crews were being given 'special treatment' which in effect was denying them their proper status as prisoners-of-war. The Captain of U-8 and his ship's company, for example, were not at first treated as POWs but kept apart, awaiting trial as pirates.

The King let Asquith know of his disapproval in no uncertain terms. He felt strongly that Great Britain should 'maintain generous and magnanimous consideration of our prisoners-of-war'. The policy was revoked, although not until Churchill and Fisher had left the Admiralty, by which time the Germans had begun to retaliate upon British POWs.

On 7th July 1915, the King visited the Grand Fleet at Scapa Flow. He arrived at 3.30 in the destroyer *Oak*. Admiral Sir Stanley Colville, Senior Officer Shetlands and Orkneys, met His Majesty in his barge. The entry was, according to Jellicoe, 'a fine sight. The *Oak* stopped and took me aboard. The King and I stood together on the bridge. We steamed all round the harbour; cold but fine. Fleet looked splendid, cheering very good. I doubt if ever he had a better reception. At 6 pm finished alongside *Druid* and had enormous tea there.'

The next morning the King arrived in Jellicoe's flagship *Iron Duke* at 9.10 and went on inspecting ships until 6.30 that evening. Jellicoe thought 'The whole thing went splendidly, 85 per cent of the officers and men passed by close to His Majesty.' The King lunched with all the Vice Admirals and there was a reception for the Captains after dinner. Before he left, the King called Jellicoe into his sleeping cabin and 'made a nice complimentary and embarrassing speech and presented me with a cigarette case.' Jellicoe, who had a sharp eye for detail, noticed that the King himself was using a cigarette case which he and other officers had given him in *Excellent* thirty years before.

On his last day the King inspected 6,000 men of the Garrison, the gunboats and the destroyers. Jellicoe formed the men in a hollow square and the King 'made an excellent speech. I called for three cheers for His Majesty, who was much affected. His visit has done an immense amount of good. The men showed extraordinary keenness. Terrible disappointment in any ships I had to send out. The whole visit was the greatest success'.

The King sent a farewell message: 'I am delighted that I have been able to carry out a long-cherished desire to visit my Grand Fleet. After two most interesting days spent here, I leave with feelings of pride and admiration for the splendid force which you command with the full confidence of myself and your fellow-countrymen. I have had the pleasure of seeing the greater portion of the officers and men of the fleet. I realise the patience and determined spirit with which you have faced long months of waiting and hoping. I know how strong is the comradeship that links all ranks together. Such a happy state of affairs convinces me that whenever the day of battle comes my Navy will add fresh triumphs to its old glorious traditions.'

Yet, when the day of battle did come, at Jutland, it did not turn out as the Navy and the country and the King had hoped. It certainly was not the great, crushing apocalyptic victory everybody had so confidently expected. The perspective of passing time has shown that the Navy did win a strategic victory at sea, but the country undoubtedly lost the ensuing propaganda battle ashore. The Germans were first with their version of events which the Admiralty communique, when it was belatedly released, seemed if anything to confirm.

The men of the Grand Fleet were amazed, and hurt, and angry. They had won a victory. They *knew* that. But everybody was behaving as though it had been a defeat. When the fleet returned to Scapa, Jellicoe sent a message of humble duty and respectful good wishes on the King's birthday, 3rd June. Perhaps he hoped that the King would respond with some morale-restoring reply.

If so, his hopes were fulfilled a thousand times over. 'I am deeply touched by the message you have sent me on behalf of the Grand Fleet,' the King said. 'It reaches me on the morrow of a battle which has once more displayed the splendid gallantry of the officers and men under your command. I mourn the loss of brave men, many of them personal friends of my own (Rear Admiral Sir Robert Arbuthnot, who was lost with everybody else in the cruiser *Defence*, had been in the King's term in *Britannia*) who have fallen in their Country's cause. Yet even more do I regret that the German High Sea Fleet, in spite of its heavy losses, was enabled by the misty weather to evade the full consequences of an encounter they have always professed to desire, but for which, when the opportunity arrived, they showed no inclination. Though the retirement of the enemy immediately after the opening of the general engagement robbed us of the opportunity of gaining a decisive victory, the events of last Wednesday amply justify my confidence in the valour and efficiency of the fleets under your command.'

A thrill of reassurance and excitement and delight swept through the fleet. Though the King could not have known at that stage any more about the battle than any member of the public through reading the papers, he unerringly put his finger on several salient points, and knew precisely where to apply the healing balm. If King George V had done nothing else for the Navy in his life, that message after Jutland would have been enough. As Admiral Sir Reginald Bacon wrote, 'it showed that the King felt, the King knew. The keen insight of the King, who had been and ever was a Naval officer, had dispelled the miasma and had assessed the battle at its true worth. Immediately a new feeling of elation swept through the fleet. Their King knew. God save the King.'

On 14th and 15th June 1916 the King visited Rosyth, Invergordon and Scapa Flow again. He stayed with Jellicoe in *Iron Duke*. By then, much more was known about the battle and the King was able to confirm personally the feelings of his Jutland message.

In December, Jellicoe went to the Admiralty as First Sea Lord. David Beatty became C-in-C of the Grand Fleet. The King sent him the perfect letter of congratulation and good wishes. 'I have known you,' he said, 'for upwards of thirty years, ever since we were shipmates together in the Mediterranean; I have watched your career with interest and admiration and I feel that the splendid fleet which you now command could not be in better hands, that you enjoy the full confidence of your officers and men, whose loyal and devoted services you can count on as surely as did your distinguished predecessor. You have my hearty good wishes and those of the whole Empire. May God bless you and my fleet and grant you victory'.

But Fisher saw dark, nefarious Royal purposes working behind Jellicoe's transfer. He told C. P. Scott it was a court intrigue. 'Kings will be cheap, as the fishmonger says of salmon sometimes'. He told Sir Edward Goulding, who had failed to be appointed head of Conservative Central Office, 'But I hear it's the King's doing associated with social drawing-room influence working with him!'

In January 1917, Fisher volunteered to serve under Jellicoe as Third Sea Lord and Controller. Jellicoe refused, clearly believing that Fisher would never be able to play third fiddle to him. Fisher was convinced it was the King who had blocked him. Fisher evidently thought that the ordinary man in the street resented the King talking about 'my Empire'. 'No King and No Class!' he wrote in October 1917. 'No one to talk of "my" Army and "my" Navy and "my" Empire.'

Yet, curiously enough, the King had just demonstrated that same month that it was not only admirals he talked to and it was not only the high and the mighty whom he entertained in his house. Lieutenant Charles Bonner RNR had won a Victoria Cross earlier in the year for outstanding bravery while First Lieutenant of the Q-ship *Dunraven*, and he had just been appointed in command of his own Q-ship. *Dunraven*'s Captain, Gordon Campbell, also a V.C., represented to the Admiralty that there was a real chance that Bonner, like another Q-ship V.C., Sanders, might be lost at sea before he could be presented with his Cross.

On Friday morning, 6th October, Bonner was in his digs in Saltash when he had a telegram telling him to report to the Fourth Sea Lord at 10 am the next day. Bonner guessed that it was an Investiture at Buckingham Palace and took with him only a small bag and his sword. But when he arrived, he was told he was to spend the weekend with the King at Sandringham.

Bonner stayed with Colonel Wigram, on the King's personal staff, who took him that evening across to York Cottage. In a letter to Campbell, Bonner said he was taken along to the King's study and left with His Majesty 'who was awfully nice. He gave me my VC, asked me a lot about you, and settled down to tell me some of his own experiences until dinner time'.

'At dinner I sat next to the King, and my opposite number, the Dean (of Norwich, another guest), next to the Queen. After the Queen, Princess Mary, and the ladies had retired, I was turned over to the Duke of York, and later taken into the drawing room to talk to the Queen'.

Next day, Bonner walked to Church with H.M., and 'was put in the front pew with Sir Dighton Probyn, V.C., he being the oldest and myself the youngest V.C.s at the moment.'

'After Church the King asked me to walk over with him to see Queen Alexandra at Sandringham House. Queen Alexandra was most gracious, and patted me on the back, and I was asked to sign her autograph book. After that I walked back with H.M. to York Cottage, and after lunch said good-bye to them all, and was motored up to King's Lynn after a most enjoyable week-end, everyone from H.M. down doing their utmost to give me a good time, especially Colonel and Mrs. Wigram, and I shall always have most happy recollections of my visit there.'

Meals at Sandringham were not lavish. From February 1917 the Royal household adhered strictly to the rationing scales then in force. The fleet, when they heard of this, felt that the King was enduring much the same hardships as themselves. There was in fact, only one point on which the King and his

Navy disagreed. On 6th April 1915, the King ordered that no wine, spirits or beer should be consumed in any of the Royal Households until the end of hostilities. The King himself became a teetotaller. This, in the Navy's almost unanimous opinion, was taking the war far too seriously.

On his next visit to the fleet in June 1917, the King inspected a 'K' Boat, one of a new class of steam-driven submarine. He held an Investiture on board *Queen Elizabeth*, Beatty's flagship. Beatty was dubbed G.C.B., Pakenham and Evan-Thomas K.C.B., Madden and Sturdee K.C.M.G. As Sir George Arthur, one of the King's biographers, wrote, 'the King was obviously and deeply moved. In the dim light — for the ceremony took place on the half-deck under shelter owing to a raging storm — his eyes shone with excitement and he spoke eagerly of the little drama which was being enacted...'

This shipboard Investiture was said to have been the first since 1794, when George III conferred an Earldom on Admiral Howe after the Glorious First of June. In fact, the King himself, when Prince of Wales, had suggested an Investiture on board the Royal Yacht *Osborne* in August 1902 after his father's Coronation. At Rosyth in 1918, the King visited the American flagship U.S.S. *New York* and, whilst on board, invested Admiral Rodman with the K.C.B. and Admiral Strauss with the K.C.M.G.

Pictures of the King and Beatty walking on the quarterdeck of *Queen Elizabeth* show clearly two friends deep in conversation. The King never had any such close relationship with Jellicoe, whom he thought too pessimistic. He made no demur when Jellicoe was dismissed at Christmas 1917. He offered him a peerage, which Jellicoe accepted, and wrote him one of his incomparable letters of consolation.

The King thought that the way Jellicoe had been removed was 'unfortunate' and told Beatty so. However, he welcomed Jellicoe's successor as First Sea Lord, his very old friend and *Britannia* term-mate 'Rosy' Wemyss. Whatever Rosy had done in the war, he had 'done *right well*', the King told him, and he had three qualities which the King thought would enable him to fill his 'very important and responsible post', namely, 'common sense, great tact, and you are an absolute gentleman.'

At last the war ground to its end, and on 12th November 1918, the King's ships took in a signal from His Majesty; 'I have remained steadfast in my confidence that whether fortune smiled or frowned, the Royal Navy would once more prove the sure shield of the British Empire in the hour of trial. Never in its history has the Royal Navy, with God's help, done greater things for us nor better sustained its old glories and the chivalry of the seas. With full and grateful hearts, the peoples of the British Empire salute the White, the Red and the Blue Ensigns, and those who have given their lives for the Flag. I am proud to have served in the Navy. I am prouder still to be its head on this memorable day.'

The post-war world into which the Navy emerged seemed in many ways unchanged. The Navy still had fleets of battleships and cruisers, with attendant destroyers, which still went on cruises, in stately progress, like a Tudor court. But it was also a time of cuts in defence expenditure, of the Geddes Axe, by which most of a generation of naval officers was forcibly dumped on the beach, to its lasting bitterness.

It was the era of the Ten Year Rule, which assumed there would be no major war at sea for at least ten years. This, of course, was the perfect excuse for doing nothing, for spending no money on design of ships or armament. It was self-perpetuating: every year it was assumed that war was ten years off (which, ironically, proved perfectly true: there was no war while the Ten Year Rule was observed, and when it was abandoned in the early 1930s there was indeed a war within ten years).

The King was by no means the dyed-in-the-wool 'big gun' conservative. He was in favour of reduced expenditure on the Navy, first advocating smaller capital ships and then their abolition. He pressed, unrealistically, for the banning of submarines, on humanitarian grounds.

The King strongly recommended that the Navy regain control of its own air arm from the RAF. He encouraged and visited the Fleet Air Arm whenever he could: for instance, in 1932 he spent a day on board the carrier *Courageous*, off Portland, with the Prince of Wales, and the Duke of York (later King George VI). The Royal party watched the flying exercises from a special vantage post built up in the island (and when they left, there was a mad rush by the rug-makers amongst *Courageous*'s sailors for the royal blue baize with which the post was lined).

Occasionally, there were painful incidents, such as the *Royal Oak* Affair, one of those (mercifully rare) occasions when the Royal Navy made an idiot of itself. A rear admiral of the Mediterranean Fleet and his flag captain, who were too close in seniority and too far apart in temperament, clashed, and there were hot words and hard words. The C-in-C, Admiral Sir Roger Keyes, ordered the rear admiral to haul down his flag, while the captain and his commander were both court-martialled, dismissed their ships and severely reprimanded.

If Keyes hoped for sympathy from the King he was disappointed. Keyes at first heard that the King was very angry. When he actually saw the King, he 'was exceedingly nice to me, but evidently thought I had made a mess of things.' The King suggested that Keyes placed too much emphasis on playing polo. Keyes said he 'had never met a keen, dashing polo-player who was not also a good officer. In the end the King agreed, and told me about his own polo days at Malta.'

Much more serious was the mutiny in ships of the Atlantic Fleet at Invergordon in September 1931. A proposed cut in pay for some members of the lower deck was appallingly maladroitly handled by the Admiralty Board. The King's solution was drastic but simple: he said 'it would be a good thing if all the Sea Lords at the time had been made to retire.'

The King never minced his words. In 1927 there was a naval conference at Geneva attended by Great Britain, the United States and Japan. The American delegation included one Admiral Hilary P. Jones, an awkward anglophobe, who aroused extreme resentment and animosity amongst the British delegates. The King followed the conference's progress closely and Lord Stamfordham reported that his comments upon Admiral Jones 'will not bear repeating'.

The King relied on the Navy for company and consolation. There was nothing he liked better than to exchange 'some salty sea stories' after dinner. After a near fatal illness in 1925 he went on a recuperative cruise round the Mediterranean in the Royal Yacht escorted by two destroyers, one of them *Vendetta*, commanded by a notable personality, Lieut. Cdr (later Captain) Walter Napier Thomason Beckett MVO DSC RN.

'Joe' Beckett (so called after the heavyweight boxer) was an Elizabethan, not to say Rabelaisian character, large of body and spirit, who was reputed to be very fond of midshipmen — preferably on toast, for breakfast. He certainly was a change from the normal run of courtier and the King vastly enjoyed his company and his conversation. Changing for dinner one evening, Joe asked Sir Derek Keppel, the King's equerry, if the

King would mind if he wore a turndown instead of a butterfly collar. The sharp points of the butterfly would dig into his neck. 'You see,' he explained to Sir Derek, 'I'm a bit of a Duckman's Chum.'

'What on earth is a Duckman's Chum?' asked the astonished Sir Derek.

'*Well*,' explained Joe, 'you know how a duck's arse begins where his head leaves off?'

That evening, while the port was going round, the King asked Joe if he always wore that sort of collar. Joe said it was a matter of putting on weight; he found it hard to get into a butterfly collar.

The King looked at him. 'That wasn't what you told Derek,' he said.

Sometimes, somebody went too far, and it was the King who put the situation right. One Senior Engineer of *Victoria and Albert* was a born clown, a superb entertainer, and a great favourite of Queen Mary's; his pantomime rendering of an old lady trying to put up a deckchair on Brighton beach used to bring tears to the Queen's eyes.

But one evening, after the Invergordon Mutiny, when the Royal Yacht was at Portland the King invited all his flag officers on board. The wardroom officers invited the admirals to the wardroom after dinner. The Senior was soon in full flow, describing with gestures the Queen having a day at sea in the King's J Class yacht *Britannia*. The weather, fine at first, grew rapidly worse and 'there was Her Majesty, holding on, her tongue all on one side — all bum and brisket...'

The Senior had let repeated success go to his head. He had not noticed how silent and pensive his audience had become. The King was standing at the back of the crowd. For a few moments a huge abyss of embarrassment yawned. But the

King burst into a great roar of laughter. 'Is that my wife you're talking about, Senior?' he said. And no more was said.

His yacht *Britannia* was the apple of the King's eye. She was built on the Clyde by D. & W. Henderson's in 1892, commissioned by the Prince of Wales (King Edward VII) who was not passionately interested in racing (certainly not like his son) but who responded to urging by his great friend Mr Willie Jameson that he might stimulate interest in big yacht racing.

Britannia had her critics, but the proof was in the racing. In five years she won 122 first prizes from 289 starts. For a time she passed out of Royal hands but was twice bought back again, the second time in 1902. As a racing skipper, King George V was nothing short of brilliant. He seemed always to know just what his boat and her crew could do in any circumstances. He had an all-seeing eye for the weather, for tactics and for his opponents. He himself was one of the best of sporting adversaries, delighted by winning, but not at all downhearted at losing. He raced *Britannia* until the end of Cowes Week in 1935, and then had her withdrawn from active sailing.

On 15th January 1936, the King felt unwell but went for a short ride on his white pony Jock in the park at Sandringham. On 20th, he apologised for keeping his Privy Council waiting at his bedside. 'I am unable to concentrate,' he said. That evening the communique was issued: 'The King's life is moving peacefully to its close.' He died at five minutes to midnight.

Seven admirals of the fleet followed the King's coffin, with naval officers from Denmark, Mexico, Greece, Peru, Finland, Sweden, Chile, Poland, France, U.S.A. and Germany (also represented by General von Runsted). Bluejackets drew the gun carriage from Westminster Hall to Paddington Station, and another team waited to draw the carriage from Windsor Station to St George's Chapel, Windsor.

There was one last funeral rite, and it was left to Joe Beckett to carry it out. At 2.43 on the morning of 10th July 1936, the yacht *Britannia* was sunk in St Catherine's deep, off the Isle of Wight, in position 50°34'18" N., 1°11'0" W, in accordance with the King's wishes.

KING GEORGE VI

His Royal Highness Prince Albert, known always to his family as 'Bertie', seemed to be unsuitable for the Navy in almost every possible way. He was a very shy boy, always liable to be nervous and tongue-tied in company, and especially in his father's company. He was extremely diffident about pushing himself forward into notice. He had a stammer which, when he was under stress, sometimes became so bad it was an agony for him and a severe embarrassment for everybody who could hear him. He was somewhat knock-kneed, not at all the athletic type of young man. It was hard to picture Bertie playing rugger or shinning up the rigging. He was not intellectually bright, indeed he seemed well below average at a great many academic subjects. His tutor at Sandringham, Mr Hansell, called him a scatterbrain who 'cannot get on without a shove'. He was not a good sailor, and certainly did not share his father's passion for the sport. He tended to suffer from stomach ailments. Fisher could speak scornfully of Prince Albert's stomach ache, but Bertie himself was to go through torments because of it.

Most fathers would have accepted that a son with such a catalogue of ailments simply was not cut out for the Navy. But King George V was not like most fathers. He himself had enjoyed the Navy, and he enjoyed it more in retrospect, as the years rolled on. He regarded the Navy as the very best kind of early training in character and discipline for any boy and especially for a prince. He was determined that his sons should join. The eldest, David, later King Edward VIII (born 23rd June 1893), Bertie (born 14th December 1895) and Prince

George, Duke of Kent (born 20th December 1902) all did so. (The third son Prince Henry, later Duke of Gloucester, served in the Army. The fifth son, Prince John, died in 1919, aged 14.)

Although the Princes loved and respected their father, they soon found out that life was very much easier at home when he was away visiting his Dominions. They quickly learned to expect a marked tightening of the screws of family work and discipline when their father returned. King George expected the highest standards of his children and was highly critical when they failed to meet his expectations. Any misdemeanour, or a bad report, incurred a thunderous and truly terrifying 'dressing down'. This bore particularly hard on Bertie. With his speech impediment he found it almost impossible to defend himself. Already shy, he tended to withdraw even more into himself.

There were no concessions to Royal rank and both boys had to take the entrance examination for the Navy. David took it successfully and went to Osborne in February 1907, as a member of the Exmouth term. Bertie studied extra hard and went for his interview on 5th November 1908. He was easily the shyest and most nervous candidate to appear — the whole Board agreed on that. He stammered badly and seemed to have the greatest difficulty in answering even the simplest question.

But, very gradually, Bertie got better as he went along. This was one of the most striking characteristics of his life; he made a slow and hesitant start, but improved dramatically when he had a little confidence. The Board persevered, gently persuaded the young man to talk about himself and the things that interested him (exactly as the Admiralty Interview Board still do to this day). Bertie grew more sure of himself, began to put thoughts and sentences together, generally began to spark up and speak up, 'brightly and well' as they said. One member said that 'if he had been a costermonger's son there would not have been the slightest hesitation in passing him'. (This was somewhat overheated hyperbole. Costermongers' sons were very thin on the ground in the wardrooms of H.M. Ships at that time. But the point is taken.)

Prince Albert sat the written examination a month later and, here again, he did much better than anybody expected: extremely well in English, History and French. His replies in the oral French examination were virtually word perfect. His mathematics was 'very fair indeed', his geometry 'below the average', but in general he passed 'most creditably'.

By the time Prince Albert joined the Navy the old *Britannia* training had been discontinued although both *Britannia* and the attendant ship *Hindostan* were still in the Dart and used for seamanship instruction; in July 1916 they were towed away and broken up for the copper in their hulls. King Edward VII had laid the foundation stone of the new College in March 1902. But as the entry age had been lowered to between 12 and 13 years (from the previous 14½ to 15½) another building was required to house the cadets during the earlier part of their course.

Part of Osborne House, on the Isle of Wight, which had been one of Queen Victoria's favourite residences (she was staying there when she died) was converted into a kind of junior annexe of Dartmouth, where the cadets spent their first two years. There, Cadet HRH Prince Albert of Wales, as he was entered on the College books, joined on 15th January 1909, as a member of the Grenville Term.

It is almost impossible for anybody today, at a time when members of the Royal Family go to school, give interviews to the media, and are seen much more often at public functions, properly to appreciate the impact Osborne must have had on

Prince Albert. Until that time he had led an extraordinarily closeted and secluded life. He had never been left to his own devices. He knew nothing of the communal life, of sleeping in a dormitory, of getting up and dressing and living with a total lack of privacy.

Until Osborne, Prince Albert had never been anywhere outside the Royal establishments, or travelled off the usual Royal itineraries. He had hardly met anybody outside the circle of Royalty, or servants and staff of Royalty. He had never sat in a class of more than three boys. He had never played organised games except the occasional closely supervised and monitored football games with Sandringham school children.

His elder brother, altogether a more outgoing and confident personality, did his best to help (although brothers were not normally encouraged to be in each other's company at Osborne or Dartmouth and indeed could only meet at certain prescribed times). Prince Edward, as he was known, wrote home that Bertie was getting on well. Bertie himself wrote, bravely, 'I have quite settled down here'.

This was quite untrue. Prince Albert was absolutely bewildered by Osborne. Life was always difficult for all new cadets, who were deliberately hurried and hustled from place to place. It took everybody time to become accustomed to the strictly limited periods allowed for getting up, for dressing, brushing one's teeth, even for saying one's prayers. Going to meals, to classes, to divisions, to chapel, was always done at the double. The two Royal princes suffered, like their father and their late uncle Albert Victor before them, from the attentions of other cadets, eager to be able to say in later life that they had personally kicked the backside of a future king or Royal duke.

Prince Albert's nervous stammer made him especially vulnerable to mockery, while senior officers, intent on discipline, often suspected insolence in a speech impediment. Altogether, it was not an easy time for Prince Albert but he was much helped by his Term Officer, Lieut. William Phipps, who made allowances for any cadet who seemed really to be trying his best, and recognised Prince Albert's additional afflictions.

As time went by, Phipps was aware that Prince Albert was a slow starter. His academic place hardly improved: he was always in the bottom five or six places, and normally 68th out of 70. Yet, in the ordinary day-to-day business of getting along with his fellows, he improved dramatically. His stammer lessened and only became noticeable when he was under pressure. He very probably was the most popular of all the Royal cadets. He never put on any 'side', never condescended, nor stood on his dignity. He took his knocks like everybody else, and he also took six of the best with the cane, for skylarking on Guy Fawkes' Day. He was already troubled by the gastric complaint which was going to make his life a misery to him in years to come. But he did not report sick. He thought the pains were bilious attacks.

His term-mates came to see there was much more to Prince Albert than first met the eye. He learned to row, and to ride, followed the Britannia beagles, and became a fair cross-country runner and an excellent left-handed tennis player. His academic place remained low. He had to submit to the most severe talking-to by his father, and the very unwelcome appearance of a tutor in his holidays.

Prince Albert was one of those unfortunate boys who seem to catch every disease going around. He had whooping cough at Osborne and he caught measles at Dartmouth. His studies were also interrupted by events such as the Royal Review in May 1912 and his father's Coronation in June. But in

December he managed to pass out of Dartmouth in 61st place, out of 68. All things are relative and this certainly was a relative improvement. 'Quite unspoiled and a nice, honest, clean-minded and excellent mannered boy,' was the report on him. 'I think he will do,' said the Captain of the College.

Prince Albert joined the training cruiser *Cumberland* with others of his term at Devonport on 17th January 1913 and the ship sailed the next day for an extended cruise to Teneriffe, the West Indies, Halifax, Quebec, and St John's, Newfoundland. King George V had stressed that his son was to be treated exactly like every other cadet. But that simply was not possible.

When people heard that Prince Albert was on board, special engagements were always arranged. He drove through the cheering streets of Teneriffe. He had to make a speech to open a new wing of the yacht club in Kingston, Jamaica. He was hunted by photographers, especially American photographers when he visited Niagara Falls. He was plagued, as all princes have been (and still are), by the girls who chased after him, swarmed up onto platforms, crowded behind him, just to touch him. After a little while, he discovered a 'look-alike' amongst the other cadets on board, who is supposed actually to have stood in successfully for the Prince at some public functions.

Cumberland returned to Devonport in July 1913 and the King was pleased to see the progress his son had made. Prince Albert had put on weight, grown in height and in assurance. He had never been a sparkling conversationalist, but he could now at least keep his end going. He suffered, as his father had done, from seasickness, which seems to have been a family affliction. The King visited *Cumberland* at Cowes after the naval manoeuvres that year and thanked Prince Albert's Term officer. 'I am pleased with my boy,' he said.

Prince Albert was promoted Midshipman on 15th September 1913 and his first appointment was the 19,500-ton battleship HMS *Collingwood*, commanded by Captain James Ley and flying the flag of King George V's old friend, Vice Admiral Sir Stanley Colville, commanding the First Battle Squadron. Like his father before him, Prince Albert lived the usual life of a midshipman, and was known on board as 'Mr Johnson'.

However, Mr Johnson could not escape the consequences of having such distinguished relatives. When *Collingwood* sailed for the Mediterranean in October 1913, Mr Johnson stayed with Lord Kitchener in Cairo, and was introduced to the Khedive of Egypt who was very impressed, just as Kitchener knew he would be, at being presented to the son of a British King. In Athens, Mr Johnson hoped to visit his cousins King Constantine of Greece and Queen Sophie but had a heavy cold. So they came on board to visit him. Mr Johnson was present at the Review of 1914 and dined on board the Royal Yacht, with sixteen admirals.

After the Review, the fleets dispersed, the ships of the First (the Grand) Fleet steaming westwards down Channel until the sun set and then turning back to the east, passing through the Straits of Dover and heading north to their war station at Scapa Flow. Prince Albert had the middle watch in *Collingwood*, from midnight to 4 am and was therefore actually on watch when war was declared. In London, his father wrote in his diary 'Please God it may soon be over & that He will protect dear Bertie's life'.

Prince Albert's particular 'part of ship' and action station was in 'A' turret, under the officer of the quarters, Lieutenant Campbell Tait, who became a personal friend. The Prince hardly had time to settle to life at Scapa Flow when, on 23rd August, he had another violent pain in his stomach. It was so bad he could hardly breathe. He went to the sickbay, where they put hot fomentations on his stomach and gave him morphia to dull the pain.

Two days later, the doctors diagnosed appendicitis and Prince Albert was moved to the hospital ship *Rohilla* at Wick. He was visited by Sir James Reid, the distinguished Scottish doctor whom the King had asked to take charge. Sir James did not feel that the Prince was well enough to be moved ashore. So Prince Albert had to endure, for the first of several times, the mortification of having to lie in bed while the fleet put to sea (on this occasion, for the action off Heligoland Bight). *Rohilla* was kept at readiness until the fleet's sortie was over. She arrived at Aberdeen on 29th August and the operation was successfully carried out on 9th September.

Prince Albert convalesced at Sandringham and then in London. It was a gloomy and rather lonely time for him. Everybody else seemed to be busy with the war. His brother the Prince of Wales had gone to France as aide-de-camp to Sir John French, the army commander. David's naval career had not lasted much longer than Dartmouth. He had passed out much higher than his younger brother, (48th out of his term of 63) but he had not gone on to the training cruiser *Cornwall* with the rest. He was three months as a midshipman in the battleship *Hindustan*, after which his active naval service was over.

But the Prince of Wales never forgot what it was to be a midshipman. In many gunrooms in the fleet, up to the outbreak of the Second World War, there were 'Gunroom Evolutions', performed by junior midshipmen, at the behest of the Sub Lieutenant and the senior midshipmen. 'Evolutions' were a form of rough, boisterous party games which more often than not took an unpleasant turn and sometimes were little better than sustained, organised bullying. All those who had to perform 'gunroom evolutions' loathed and dreaded them.

The battlecruiser *Renown*, in which the Prince of Wales went on a cruise to India and Japan in 1921–22, had a 'tough gunroom'. When the Prince dined in the gunroom as a guest of the mess somewhere in the Indian Ocean, according to Midshipman J. Litchfield, 'it was whispered that gunroom evolutions on this occasion would be a royal gala performance. When dinner was finished the senior Sub., with a rather sinister smile, asked H.R.H. if he would care to see the junior midshipmen perform. 'By all means,' he replied, remembering his own experiences as a junior snotty, 'that is, of course, if *all* my hosts take part'. A silence fell upon his senior hosts, and no more was heard of the suggestion. His junior hosts long remembered this royal reprieve with gratitude.

Inactivity weighed very heavily on Prince Albert. He felt it very deeply that other midshipmen, some of them in his own term, had seen action against the enemy. He was relieved to be given a job in the Admiralty, keeping charts up to date and generally making himself useful in the War Room. 'Nobody will be able to say that I am doing nothing,' he wrote to his mother.

Another action, on the Dogger Bank, took place in January 1915, when Prince Albert was still languishing on shore. He began to suffer the depths of depression again. He found office life monotonous and meaningless. 'Nothing to do as usual' he kept on writing in his diary, for day after day.

The King's own surgeon, Sir Frederick Treves, thought that Prince Albert should not go to sea again. But the Prince kept on pressing, and arguing that he felt well enough. Eventually he succeeded in convincing the Second Sea Lord and, to his great joy, rejoined *Collingwood* at Portsmouth on 12th February 1915.

Prince Albert was now no longer a 'junior wart', but one of the senior midshipmen. His night action station was in charge of the searchlights. By day he supervised the submarine lookouts. For three months, his health was very good. But early in May 1915, the dreaded symptoms returned, with violent stomach spasms of pain, sickness and vomiting — the 'infernal indigestion' as he called it. The doctors who had said he should never go to sea again were vindicated (however, those same distinguished physicians had absolutely no grounds to congratulate themselves; they all got the ultimate diagnosis utterly wrong).

Prince Albert recovered from his first attacks well enough to be able to greet his father, when the King visited the Grand Fleet from 7th to 9th July 1915. But it was only a respite. On 12th July he was taken to the hospital ship *Drina*. Somebody from *Collingwood* came to visit him every day and he was able to carry on his studies for the rank of Acting Sub-Lieutenant. Most encouraging of all, his father, his captain, and the doctors had assured him that if the Fleet ever put to sea for action, he would be allowed to return to *Collingwood*.

The trouble had been diagnosed as a weakening of the stomach wall. The treatment was a quiet undisturbed life, careful diet, and the artificial emptying of the stomach before sleep every night. With that regime, there was a chance of improvement. It was not much of a life or a prognosis for a keen young man of nineteen, but Prince Albert made the best of it.

After a month, he was making progress, but not such good progress as all that. Poor Captain Ley was in a quandary. The doctors did not think Prince Albert should ever return to active service and Ley agreed with them. But if he took *Collingwood* to sea and into action without the Prince he would be breaking his word to the Prince and to the King.

Captain Ley wrote to the King to explain his dilemma. King George thought what he himself would have done, had he been in his son's position. He had no doubt that he would have wished to go to sea, no matter what the result. The only alternative would be to declare finally that his son was unfit for service. That, the King absolutely refused to do. He therefore replied that risks had to be taken with his son's health.

King George V was never as close to his sons as he himself had been to his own father Edward VII. But their correspondence suggests that the procession of events in wartime brought the King and Prince Albert a good deal closer together. Now, in a moment of rare *rapport*, the King saw clearly that it would be a shattering emotional blow to Bertie to miss 'The Day' when the German fleet at last came out, and all because of this silly illness, as he thought of it, which was no more than bilious indigestion. Only an ex-naval officer like King George V could have insisted that such a seemingly unsuitable son should have joined the Navy in the first place. Ironically, only an ex-naval officer could have understood now what it meant to his son to be able to stay in the Navy.

Actually, nothing changed. The King wrote through Lord Stamfordham that he hoped Prince Albert would continue to progress every day and be able to return to duty before 'The Day' arrived. In fact, the Prince was always making 'satisfactory progress' but never seemed to become fit for sea. He went to the Highlands for eight weeks' recuperation. The news of his father's horrible accident, when his mare threw him and fell on top of him, delayed his route to recovery. The Naval Medical Board took a bleakly realistic view, refused to allow him to rejoin his ship and granted him three months' sick leave, which he did not want. Prince Albert went to France to visit his brother and in March 1916 began his Royal duties with his first official engagement: the opening of a new rifle range at the Houses of Parliament.

Prince Albert was promoted Acting Sub Lieutenant on 15th September 1915 and was confirmed in the rank on 15th May 1916. By then, he had rejoined *Collingwood* (on 5th May). He was fit and well, his sickness apparently behind him. Yet, when the Grand Fleet put to sea on the evening of 30th May, Prince Albert was once again in the sickbay — suffering from over-indulgence in 'soused herrings' at supper in *Invincible* two nights before!

But the news that the German fleet was out acted as the best tonic in the world. 'Huge excitement,' Lieutenant Tait told the Prince of Wales. 'Out at last. Full speed ahead. Sound of "Action" — you can imagine the scene! Out of his bunk leaps "Johnson". Ill? Never felt better! Strong enough to go to his turret and fight a prolonged action? Of course he was, why ever not?'

Prince Albert sent home a vivid account of Jutland, seen through a midshipman's eyes. 'We went to Action Stations at 4.30 pm. and saw the Battle Cruisers in line ahead of us on the starboard bow. As we came up the *Lion*, leading our Battle Cruisers, appeared to be on fire the port side of the forecastle, but it was not serious. They turned up to starboard so as not to cross the bows of the Fleet. As far as one could see only 2 German battle squadrons and all their Battle Cruisers were out. The *Colossus* leading the 6th Division with the *Collingwood* her next astern were nearest the enemy. The whole Fleet deployed at 5.0 and opened out. We opened fire at 5.37 pm. on some German light cruisers. The *Collingwood*'s second salvo hit one of them which set her on fire, and sank after two more salvoes were fired into her. We then shifted on to another light cruiser and helped to sink her as well. Our next target was a battle cruiser, we think the *Derrflinger* or *Lutzow*, and one of the *Collingwood*'s salvoes hit her abaft the after turret, which burst into a fierce flame. After this she turned away from us and disappeared into the mist.'

'I was in A turret,' wrote Prince Albert, 'and watched most of the action through one of the trainer's telescopes, as we were firing by Director, when the turret is trained in the working chamber and not in the gunhouse. At the commencement I was sitting on top of A turret and had a very good view of the proceedings. I was up there during a lull, when a German ship started firing at us, and one salvo "straddled" us. We at once returned the fire. I was distinctly startled and jumped down the hole in the top of the turret like a shot rabbit! I didn't try the experience again! The ship was in a fine state on the main deck. Inches of water sluicing about to prevent fires from getting a hold on the deck. Most of the cabins were also flooded.

'The hands behaved splendidly and all of them in the best of spirits as their hearts' desire had at last been granted, which was to be in action with the Germans. Some of the turret's crew actually took on bets with one another that we should not fire a shot. A good deal of money must have changed hands I should think by now.'

'My impressions were very different to what I expected. I saw visions of the masts going over the side and funnels hurtling through the air etc. In reality none of these things happened and we are still quite as sound as before. No one would know to look at the ship that we had been in action. It was certainly a great experience to have been through and it shows that we are at war and that the Germans can fight if they like.'

'By this time it was too dark to fire and we went to Night Defence stations. The 4" guns were manned to repel destroyer attacks. Our 12" firing was very good, though rather slow, as we could only fire at the flashes of the German guns. The range at the commencement was 10,000 yards and ceased at 8,000 yards. The Germans fired some of their torpedoes but only one of them took effect in the *Marlborough*, the flagship of the 1st Battle Squadron... One torpedo passed ahead of the *Collingwood* and another astern. We had no casualties and no damage was done to us, though we were "straddled" several times... We were not attacked at all during the night and everything was very quiet.'

Petty Officer James Moffatt, the gunlayer in A turret, who shared the whole experience with the Prince, has also left an account of Jutland. 'Prince Albert had taken advantage of a lull in the fighting to climb through a hole on to the roof.

'Soon a salvo screamed overhead, and the officer of the gun-turret glanced up anxiously.

'What the hell are you doing out there?' he cried. 'Come down before you get your head blown off.'

'The air in our gun-turret was poisonous with the fumes of burnt cordite and of hot oil, and the smell of paint blistering on overheated guns. Suddenly the mist-screen lifted leaving us open to the enemy fire. Exposed to danger from bursts and splinters, Prince Albert ducked as the shells shrieked by and tumbled back into the turret.

"Whew, that was a near thing, Moffatt," he said. "The blighters have straddled us."

'...Prince Albert returned to his small stool, which was next to my own in the 'Silent' or Control Cabinet, at the rear of the turret. Before us were fire-control instruments, dependent upon each other and extremely technical, one called the Dumaresque, which was worked by Prince Albert, the other the Clock, which was my responsibility. The Prince became intent upon his work. Every now and again his eyes turned to the floor where there was a small circular hole about four inches in diameter. Through this hole a brass plate bearing numbers, sometimes in red, sometimes in green, according to position, could be clearly defined. Presently numbers showed green.

"'Green-nine-o" called out the Prince, loud enough to be heard above the din of preparation and the hissing of the hydraulic gear in the gunhouse. "Green-ninety", I confirmed, turning my own instrument to the appropriate mark.

'It was a relief to be in the thick of the battle. At once we forgot our discomforts, and our nerves from being a trifle frayed became calm and in first-class working order. We settled down to the work in hand, everything running as smoothly as though we were engaged in a practice shoot instead of with an enemy who was doing his utmost to sink us.'

However, there were distractions. 'We were sitting side by side at our instruments when a young midshipman, who was stationed in the gunhouse, ran into the Control Cabinet.'

"'Prince Albert," he cried, a little breathlessly, "if you get killed can I have the silver in your pocket as a memento?"

'Prince Albert seemed astounded and for a moment puzzled just how to receive this particular request. Then he said a little abruptly: "No, you can't." He turned to me. There was a suspicion of a smile upon his face as he said: "If I get hit you can have the cash, Moffatt."

"'If you get hit *I* can have it! I like that!" I exclaimed.

"'Why?" asked the Prince.

'"Well, because the shell that hits you hits me!"

'"Of course, of course", he said, and burst out laughing.'

Later… 'came tragedy. We passed a ship on the port hand. She was blown apart. The bows and stern protruded from the water. Thinking that she was an enemy vessel which the ships ahead had sunk, we cheered. Prince Albert gazed hard at the stricken ship. He had a good view. He did not cheer, and I believe he knew the truth. The sinking ship was our own *Invincible*. We saw men in the water, hanging on to the wreckage.'

In all Prince Albert's later accounts and memories of Jutland, his constant theme was 'Thank *God* I was back in time.' He was not afraid. 'When I was on top of the turret I never felt any fear of shells or anything else.' he told his brother. 'It seems curious but all sense of danger and everything else goes except the one longing of dealing death in every possible way to the enemy'. The Prince had proved himself in action and, whatever else happened now, he had at least been *there* on the day and done his share.

He was shortly to need all the reassurance he could get. 'I really think now that I have got over all my inside troubles,' he told his father in July. But on the evening of 26th August he felt the familiar shooting pains in his abdomen. His old enemy was back. He was taken ashore to the Naval Hospital at South Queensferry and, soon afterwards, to Windsor. He had, as it turned out, left *Collingwood* for good.

The complaint was diagnosed as a duodenal ulcer which needed a long period of rest. In the meantime, Prince Albert was appointed to the staff of the C-in-C Portsmouth, Admiral Sir Stanley Colville. He renewed his acquaintance with submarines (like aircraft, a constant preoccupation of his family). He and Charles Cust went out for the day in K.3 and, like his father, he had to endure an awkward moment. The submarine dived and stuck its nose in the mud of the Solent for fifteen minutes before coming free again. Somebody had forgotten to flood a forward tank with the rest, and when it finally was flooded, the submarine went down with a rush. The submarine's CO must have been highly embarrassed. But the Prince thought it 'most interesting and a great experience'.

Prince Albert was made a Knight of the Garter by his father on his 21st birthday, 14th December 1916, while he was on leave at Buckingham Palace. Early the next summer, his health seemed to have improved enough for him to join another ship, the 27,500-ton battleship *Malaya*, (Captain the Hon. Algernon Boyle) on 8th May 1917, with the rank of acting lieutenant. There were some old friends on board, including Campbell Tait, now a Commander, and Louis Greig, the ship's assistant surgeon, whom Prince Albert had first met at Osborne. Greig played a tremendous part in helping and cheering Prince Albert through his periods of sickness. He and the Prince became the greatest of friends: '... a perfect topper', the Prince once called him.

The Prince began to enjoy naval life again, but it was not to last. He was laid up with another gastric attack on 26th July, and ten days later he was transferred to the South Queensferry Hospital. His great-uncle the Duke of Connaught visited him there and found him very thin, and ill, and deeply depressed. This really was the end. The Prince himself decided, in a characteristically honest and brave decision, that he could not go on in the Navy, much as he loved it. 'Personally I feel that I am not fit for service at sea,' he told his father, 'even when I recover from this little attack.'

This did not mean the end of an active life. The Prince decided he would learn to fly, and he was appointed to the

Royal Naval Air Service Station at Cranwell on 13th November 1917. The Prince was surprised that approval was given so readily. 'My own suggestion for once came off and Papa jumped at the idea,' he said.

But first he must have the operation. It was carried out on 29th November and was a complete success. The cause of all the trouble the Prince had had since 1915 was found and cured. If only a correct diagnosis had been made earlier, the Prince would have stayed in the Navy and his whole life would have been different. He had served in the Navy for three years and eleven months, from September 1913 until August 1917. He had been at sea for twenty-two months: in *Collingwood* for three periods, from September 1913 to August 1914, from February to July 1915, and May to August 1916; and in *Malaya* from May to August 1917.

As one member of the family left the Navy, another joined. Prince Albert's younger brother George, later Duke of Kent, had just gone to Dartmouth as a cadet. He left in May 1920, to join the training cruiser *Temeraire*. Prince Albert noted gleefully that George 'has kept up the best traditions of my family by passing out of Dartmouth 1 from bottom, the same place as I did!!!!' The Prince himself joined HMS *Daedalus*, the air station at Cranwell in Lincolnshire, some 12 miles north-east of Grantham, on 1st January 1918.

Cranwell had been a base for operational airships and became a great training base for aeroplane and airships crews. It was a different life to anything the Prince had known. He was assistant to the adjutant, and O.C. of Boys Training. He thought his fellow officers 'very nice, though a curious mixture of people, in every walk of life.' He found a 'tremendous difference' between the petty officers of the R.N.A.S. and what he called 'the proper Naval P.O.' He hoped to make them understand what he wanted 'with a little persuasion'.

It was a happy time. The Prince rode, played tennis, learned to drive a car. Louis Greig and his wife had taken a cottage nearby. He had his first flight which he found a 'curious sensation'. He enjoyed it 'on the whole, but I don't think I should like flying as a pastime,' he told his mother. 'I would much sooner be on the ground!! It feels safer!!'

When the Royal Air Force achieved its independence as a service on 1st April 1918 Prince Albert became a Flight Lieutenant. On 11th, his father and mother visited Cranwell and the O.C. Boys watched his charges, some 2,500 of them, parade before Their Majesties. The Royal Party toured the station 'inspected the boys whom Bertie is in charge of', saw all the different types of aircraft and the airships in their sheds, but it was too misty and foggy for any flying.

Despite his mixed feelings about flying, Prince Albert was determined to get his wings and began training at Croydon in March 1919, with Lieutenant (later Air Chief Marshal Sir William) Coryton as his instructor. He passed his Modified Test at Croydon on 28th July, his air and ground tests three days later and received his wings on 31st July 1919. He was promoted to Squadron Leader the next day. He had set a Royal standard. His brothers, the Prince of Wales, Prince Henry the Duke of Gloucester, Prince George Duke of Kent, his son-in-law the Duke of Edinburgh, and his two grandsons the Prince of Wales and Prince Andrew, all learned to fly. But he was the first fully qualified pilot in the Royal Family and, till now, the only Sovereign to win fully-entitled wings.

Prince Albert became a Wing Commander on 1st June 1920, Group Captain on 30th June 1921, Air Chief Marshal on 21st January 1936, and Marshal of the Royal Air Force on his accession to the throne, 11th December 1936. Similarly, he was promoted Commander on 31st December 1920, Captain on 30th June 1925, Rear Admiral on 3rd June 1932, Vice Admiral 1st January, Admiral 21st January and Admiral of the Fleet, 11th December 1936.

In July 1919 Prince Albert virtually gave up his Service career, to go to Cambridge for a year 'to learn everything that will be useful for the time to come'. He could already see that his brother was overwhelmed with work and made up his mind to help him in every way he could. On 3rd June 1920 he was made Duke of York, Earl of Inverness and Baron Killarney, and first took his seat in the House of Lords on 23rd. From now on, he became a full-time hard-working member of the Royal Family, although he visited naval ships whenever he could.

In 1921 the Duke fell in love with Elizabeth Bowes-Lyon, ninth child of the Earl of Strathmore, and became engaged to her on 15th January 1923. The couple were married at a service of great splendour in Westminster Abbey on 26th April 1923 and, as they say, lived happily ever after. Their first child, Elizabeth, was born at their home 17 Bruton Street, London W1, on 21st April 1926.

But before their eldest child was a year old, the Duke and Duchess had to leave on Royal business. They sailed from Portsmouth in the battlecruiser *Renown* (Captain N. A. Sulivan) on 6th January 1927, for a tour of Australia and New Zealand. *Renown*, in which the Prince of Wales had already visited Canada in 1919, Australia and New Zealand in 1920, and India and the Far East in 1921–22, and her sister ship *Repulse*, in which the Prince of Wales visited West and South Africa and South America in 1925, were well suited for Royal passengers

— much better than the Royal Yacht *Victoria and Albert*, which was strictly for Cowes and Reviews.

Both ships had a self-contained suite of spacious, airy cabins in the after superstructure, which were free of vibration and where the scuttles could be open at sea in any weather. In *Renown*, a triple 4-inch gun mounting was removed from the port waist to make space for a timber squash court, and a 'sort of pulpit', decorated with the Royal Arms (which the irreverent said should have been inscribed 'By Appointment') was built above the bridge, for the Royal party when entering or leaving harbour.

The Australian tour of 1927 was a great success for *Renown*. According to Lieutenant John Litchfield, the Royals 'were a jolly party and life with them on board was fun. But there were as they say, moments. The first came during scrub decks after a very hot night at sea, when shrieks were heard coming from the royal suite, whose scuttles looked out on the waist deck. The Immortals, as the royal passengers were known in the wardroom, and their staff appeared in dressing gowns, mingling among the fore-topmen hosing down the deck, and soon the ship's top brass arrived in a great tizzy'.

'It transpired that the Duchess of York's personal maid — a lady who gave herself more than royal airs and was inclined to boss the Navy about — had become overheated during the night and had been sleeping with a fan playing on her upperworks and her bare feet cooling in the open scuttle. A seaman on the scrub outside could not resist the temptation: he tweaked her big toe. Nobody thought it funnier than her mistress. "Very good for her!", she remarked.'

Renown's ship's company had been warned beforehand that there were ladies on board and language must be restrained. But there were very occasional occasions 'which provoke the most saintly characters to use meaningful language'. The Royal party, ladies and all, had gathered on deck to watch a lifebuoy being dropped and the sea-boat being sent away to pick it up. All went well until the sea-boat came back and several dozen sailors manned the falls, ready to hoist, to the beat of a massed band. But on the way up, the falls took a twisted turn and soon began to look like 'a bunch of bananas'. The order 'Vast hauling' had no effect. Nothing could be heard above the band.

'Then from immediately above the Royal Party a voice spoke — meaningfully and screamingfully. The Commander had both a voice trained on the parade ground of Whale Island and a vocabulary which even hardened seamen admired, and he drew upon it without reserve. He even silenced the band; and what an admiral said to the bandmaster of the *Royal Oak* on another famous occasion a year later was quite parliamentary compared to the language which was heard over the length and breadth of the Pacific Ocean that afternoon.'

'The Royal Party, looking somewhat cowed, moved aft in silence, and Field Marshal the Earl of Cavan, the Chief of Staff, complained about the Navy's language'.

The Duke, of course, was thoroughly at home on board. He took part in the ceremony of Crossing the Line, although in fact he had already crossed the Equator on passage to East Africa and the Sudan in the P. & O. liner *Mulbera* in December 1924. Afterwards, the Duke found a very frayed piece of rope, somewhat ostentatiously laid out on deck. 'What's this?' he asked. 'That, sir,' was the reply, 'is the main-brace.' 'It needs splicing,' said the Duke, manfully playing his part. 'Make it so.'

When the Duke returned in June, he resumed his role in the Royal Family. He had an abiding interest in young people and his Duke of York camps for boys were famous. He became

Lord High Commissioner of the General Assembly of the Church of Scotland, an appropriate office in view of his family's long connection with Scotland. But the Duke of York might have lived the rest of his life as a very well-known, very well-liked and respected, but minor, figure on the periphery of Royal life and the doings of the country. This is what he himself would have preferred.

The Abdication of Edward VIII changed everything. The shy, willing, but unassuming Duke of York became King overnight, *malgré lui*. His father had never initiated him into the ordinary working of government, but he had seen the crushing volume of papers which descended upon a King. He knew roughly what the job meant, but he had no idea how to do it. He was appalled by the prospect.

On the very first night of his reign, he and Lord Louis Mountbatten were at Fort Belvedere, while the ex-King was preparing to leave. 'Dickie, this is absolutely terrible, I never wanted this to happen,' he said. 'I'm quite unprepared for it. David has been trained for this all his life. I've never even seen a State paper. I'm only a naval officer, it's the only thing I know about.'

Whereupon, Lord Louis made what was, from the Navy's point of view, a most significant and revealing remark. 'This is a very curious coincidence,' he said. 'My father once told me that, when the Duke of Clarence died, your father came to him and said almost the same things that you have said to me now, and my father answered: "George, you're wrong. There is no more fitting preparation for a King than to have been trained in the Navy".'

King George VI soon showed that this was true enough. As at Dartmouth, he demonstrated that he was a slow and hesitant starter, but he was a sure finisher. He gained confidence as he went along, expanding his capability to meet the demands on him, and he was prepared to persevere until the end. In the spring of 1939, the King and Queen visited Canada. They should have gone in *Repulse*, but the King felt that, with such a delicate international situation, using a powerful capital ship for such a purpose might show that Great Britain did not mean business.

The Admiralty at first demurred but then agreed, and the liner *Empress of Australia* was specially chartered. For the purposes of this trip she was treated as a Royal Yacht, entitled to fly the White Ensign, with the King himself in supreme command, and Vice Admiral Sir Dudley North commanding the whole Royal Squadron. They sailed on 5th May, with *Repulse* escorting them halfway across the Atlantic. After delays due to thick fog they arrived in Quebec on 17th May.

After Canada, the King went on to the United States in June, the first reigning British sovereign ever to visit the ex-colony. In Canada and the U.S.A. the King made an astoundingly successful personal impression. He must have had an incalculable effect upon President Roosevelt and on his opinion of the British Isles.

Once home, the King followed his success abroad with a speech at the Guildhall on the ideals of the Commonwealth which staggered and delighted his audience. For one magic evening, the tongue-tied Bertie was given the golden tongue of an orator. Where he had always stammered, the King now soared, in a speech which warned Europe that Britain meant to stand by her old ideals, which reassured and warmed the country's friends in America, and reminded the Commonwealth of their family responsibilities. The King himself took the unaccustomed acclaim modestly enough. 'It was a change from the old days,' he admitted, 'when speaking, I felt, was *hell.*'

The last days of the summer of 1939, the last of the old world, slipped away. On 9th August the King inspected the Reserve Fleet at Weymouth. He was very impressed. 'It is wonderful the way in which all the men have come back for duty at this time,' he said. He sent them a signal ordering them to Splice the Mainbrace and saying what a great pleasure it had been to inspect them and that he realised what sacrifices the retired officers, pensioners and reservists had made in leaving their work and homes to make such a quick and important addition to the country's naval strength. 'If we can only get through these 2 months without a crisis,' he wrote to Queen Mary, 'all would be well.'

It was a vain hope. At the outbreak of war, the King started to keep a diary. His thoughts inevitably went back to the previous occasion, when he was a midshipman keeping the middle watch in *Collingwood* at sea. 'I was 18 years of age. In the Grand Fleet everyone was pleased that it had come at last… We were not prepared for what we found a modern war really was, and those of us who had been through the Great War never wanted another. Today we are at War again, and I am no longer a midshipman in the Royal Navy.'

In the first week of October 1939 the King visited the fleet, just as his father had done in the previous war, at Invergordon and Scapa Flow. There lay the great ships at anchor, their massive turrets and fighting tops silhouetted against the gorgeous clear skies and sunsets of Scapa Flow (mercifully the fierce winds of Scapa were absent).

Things were not quite the same. The King dined with the flag officers in the flagship *Nelson.* 'Not quite such a number as there were in the Great War when Papa came to visit the

Grand Fleet,' he noted. He inspected the ship's company of the cruiser *Effingham*, the sailors marching past individually and saluting, just as the sailors of a previous generation had saluted his father. 'I was very interested to see things as they are at the beginning of a war,' he said. 'In rather a muddle, but it is amazing how the Services put up with things, and carry on under trying conditions.'

There was rather more of a muddle than the King thought. Incredibly, in view of the Navy's experience in the first war, the anchorage at Scapa was once again open to submarine attack. Only a few days after the King, Scapa had another visitor. On 13th October, Leutnant Prien in U-47 penetrated the Flow and sank the battleship *Royal Oak*.

On 19th December the King visited Portsmouth. It was a very cold day, but His Majesty set a hot pace. He went to HMS *Vernon*, the anti-submarine and torpedo school, to decorate the men who had stripped the magnetic mine on the mudflats off Shoeburyness and revealed its secrets: DSOs to Lt. Cdr. John Ouvry and Lt. Cdr. R. C. Lewis, DSMs to C.P.O. Baldwin and A. B. Vearncombe.

When the King arrived at the Barracks, the parade ground was empty but at a signal thousands of men poured out of an underground shelter and fell in by their divisions. The parade included hundreds of reservists who had rejoined the Colours. As the King walked round the C-in-C Admiral Sir William James said to him: 'I have something to show you sir, that you have never seen before — twelve dentists standing shoulder to shoulder!'

It was to be a bitterly cold winter, the coldest for many years and at the Royal Marine Barracks, Eastney, the wind off the sea was so cutting, the programme was curtailed and the King went early into the officers' mess. He was asked to sign his name in the visitors' book, but the inkwell was empty. 'The Marine officers' faces would have delighted H. M. Bateman' said Admiral James, delightedly.

The King visited the Wrens and commented that many of them were not wearing uniform. He went round the galleys of the Barracks, manned by sailors' wives and daughters, and said he thought the work was too rough for them. He had tea at Whale Island and came back to Admiralty House where Lady James had a Christmas tree and a party for wives and children. The King went into the drawing room to join in the games and the fun.

Admiral James had a keen eye for a story and knew the benefits of good publicity (he later became Chief of Naval Information) and he was one of the first to recognise the enormous morale-boosting effect of the King's visits. The King was as indefatigable a traveller as his father. He went to France, like his father, and to hospitals and to individual units. The newspapers and the magazines of the day showed him, often in his naval greatcoat with Admiral of the Fleet's shoulder straps, or in his British Warm overcoat, endlessly shaking hands, stepping down from trains or out of cars (later the cars were armoured), endlessly inspecting guards of honour — of sailors, Canadians, New Zealanders, paratroopers, the Women's Land Army, Highlanders, Local Defence Volunteers, (when they were LDVs and again when they became the Home Guard).

The King and Queen were shown picking their way amongst rubble, watching women in mob caps sewing seams or filling shells, talking to officers of the Metropolitan Police, watching a firefighting demonstration by the Auxiliary Fire Service, sipping cups of tea from a mobile YMCA tea van, chatting with old ladies standing on the doorsteps of their bomb-shattered houses, listening to a lunchtime recital by Myra Hess at the National Gallery.

Their Majesties had their own bomb damage and were shown in the courtyard of Buckingham Palace surveying the effects of a bomb which had come much too close for the nation's peace of mind. They went to the Union Jack Club, they went to the Clyde, to Birkenhead, to Lancashire, to Dover, to the East End, to Coventry, to Aldershot. The King and Queen were part of a nation at war and today it is hard to look at some of those pictures — the children in their gas masks, the old man with his medals beside his garden gate, the A.R.P. warden grinning under his steel helmet, the drawn faces of the crowds on the underground station platforms — without being moved close to tears.

Unconsciously, the King projected the most marvellously reassuring image of confidence and serenity. He was solemn but always ready to chuckle, concerned but cheerful. His Christmas broadcast of 1939, which he practised furiously beforehand, praying that his stammer would not spoil it, was a message of hope. 'A new year is at hand. We cannot tell what it will bring. If it brings peace, how thankful we shall all be. If it brings us continued struggle we shall remain undaunted. In the meantime I feel that we may all find a message of encouragement in the lines which, in my closing words, I would like to say to you:- "'I said to the man who stood at the Gate of the Year, 'Give me a light that I may tread safely into the unknown'. And he replied, 'Go out into the darkness, and put your hand into the Hand of God. That shall be to you better than light, and safer than a known way.'" May that Almighty Hand guide and uphold us all.'

The King's quotation caused a great deal of interest and curiosity. Part of a poem in a collection of verse called *The*

Desert, published privately in 1908 by Miss Marie Louise Haskins, a lecturer at the London School of Economics, it was sent to the King shortly before his broadcast and he at once saw its aptness.

The winter seemed interminable. But, in Arctic weather, the King kept up his programme. On 6th February 1940, he was in the West Country, on 15th he presented Colours to the Irish Guards at Wellington Barracks, on 21st he was inspecting Wrens at Chatham, on 23rd inspecting the officers and men of the cruisers *Exeter* and *Ajax*, who, with *Achilles*, had outmanoeuvred and outfought the German battleship *Graf Spee* off the River Plate the previous December, on 26th he was in Glasgow and on 28th touring Clydeside shipyards.

In May 1940, with the German successes in Norway and the Low Countries, and the impending defeat of France, the King sensed that one of the war's great climacterics was approaching. He had as acute a sense of what people were thinking as any politician. In his Empire Day speech on 24th May he began 'The decisive struggle is now upon us...' He ended: 'So now, peoples of the Empire, men and women in all parts of the globe, I say to you: Put into your task, whatever it may be, all the courage and purpose of which you are capable. Keep your hearts proud and your resolve unshaken. Let us go forward to that task as one man, a smile on our lips and our heads held high, and with God's help we shall not fail.'

In July the King paid another visit to Portsmouth and, once again, Admiral James was ready with a busy programme. It happened to be the day after a damaging 'blitz' on the town and the dockyard workers gave the King 'a roaring reception'. There were no bombproof shelters on the King's route and the Admiral was glad when they completed the programme without interference from German aircraft.

On parade this time were French, Dutch, Polish and Norwegian sailors 'and at every turn a British officer or sailor wearing a medal for gallantry, which never failed to catch the King's eye. His visit did much good,' wrote Admiral James.

The King took a great interest in medals and decorations, like his father. On 3rd September 1940, the war's first anniversary, the King invested Lieut. Richard Stannard RNR with his Victoria Cross, gained for great gallantry in command of the trawler *Arab* at Namsos in April and May during the Norwegian campaign. It was not the first naval Victoria Cross of the war; Warburton-Lee and Mantle were earlier, but both were posthumous. It was not the earliest dated V.C. of the war: Roope had rammed the German cruiser *Hipper* in his destroyer *Glowworm* in April; but Roope was dead, *Glowworm*'s survivors were in German POW camps, and their story would not be known until after the war. Thus Stannard was the first naval VC of the war to receive his Cross from the King. In November 1940, after the epic fight of the armed merchant cruiser *Jervis Bay* with the German battleship *Admiral Scheer*, the King himself insisted on awarding a posthumous Victoria Cross to her captain, Fogarty Fegen.

By this time, the King had recognised that many civilians had conducted themselves with great bravery, though not in the presence of the enemy. During the blitz, for example, many civilians were in the front line in everything but name. The King took great pleasure in planning every detail of a new decoration, and made several sketches of it.

The King announced the creation of the George Cross in a broadcast to the nation on the evening of 23rd September 1940. He said: 'Many and glorious are the deeds of gallantry done during these perilous but famous days. In order that they should be worthily and promptly recognised, I have decided to create at once a new mark of honour to this new distinction which will consist of the George Cross. It will rank next to the Victoria Cross.'

A second Royal Warrant of 21st January 1941 laid down that surviving holders of the Empire Gallantry Medal (instituted by King George V in 1922) and men and women who had won the EGM posthumously since the outbreak of war, should have their EGMs replaced by the George Cross.

Amongst the very earliest George Cross winners were Sub. Lt. W. H. Taylor, RNVR, C.P.O. R. V. Ellingworth, Lt. Cdr. R. J. H. Ryan, Sub. Lt. P. V. Danckwerts RNVR, Sub. Lt. J. M. C. Easton RNVR, Ordinary Seaman B. Southwell, Lt. R. S. Armitage RNVR, Sub. Lt. R. V. Moore RNVR, Sub. Lt. J. H. Babington RNVR, Lt. H. R. Newgass RNVR, Sub. Lt. F. H. Brooke-Smith RNVR, Sub. Lt. G. G. Turner RNVR, Sub. Lt. J. B. P. Miller RNVR, Able Seaman S. J. Tuckwell, and Lt. E. O. Gidden RNVR, all for bomb or mine disposal in the last few months of 1940 or the beginning of 1941. In April 1942, the King awarded the George Cross to the island of Malta.

King George VI did not confer the same number of awards and decorations, particularly of VCs, as his father. But on 7th July 1942 at Buckingham Palace the King held a remarkable and quite unprecedented Investiture at which Cdr. A. C. C. Miers, commanding the submarine HMS *Torbay*, received a Victoria Cross, Lt.(E) Hugh Kidd a DSO, Lts. Paul Chapman and D. S. Verschoyle-Campbell DSCs, and twenty-four ratings of *Torbay* received DSMs or Bars to their DSMs.

In the spring and summer of 1942 the King visited Scottish, Eastern, Southern and Bomber Commands, Northern Ireland and Scapa, and on 30th September, Portsmouth again, on Admiral James' last day as C-in-C. The Admiral had laid on another full programme, including a 'steam-past' of 25 coastal craft of six different types. The Admiral wrote, expressing the feelings of all those visited by the King in those days, 'he was most kind and appreciative; it is impossible to over-estimate the value of his four visits to Portsmouth. He was so genuinely interested in all he saw, and so natural when talking to men and women that they were always responsive; hundreds treasure the memory of a talk with their King.'

On 25th August 1942, a Coastal Command Sunderland on its way to Iceland crashed in the highlands of Scotland. Only the rear gunner survived and amongst those killed was Rear Admiral HRH the Duke of Kent. Prince George had left the Navy because of ill health in 1929, when he had served as Midshipman in *Iron Duke*, as a Lieutenant in the cruiser *Hawkins* in the China Station, in *Nelson* in the Atlantic Fleet and in the cruiser *Durban* on the American and West Indies Station. In 1927 he went to Canada with the Prince of Wales.

In 1940 the Duke had turned over to the RAF and was in fact Chief Welfare Officer, RAF Home Command, with the rank of Air Commodore, when he was killed. He had visited dozens of air stations up and down the country. In 1941 he became the first member of the Royal Family to fly the Atlantic when he went to inspect air force establishments in Canada and the United States.

HRH the Duchess of Kent, Princess Marina, had been Commandant of the WRNS since the outbreak of war, and took her duties very seriously. She too, tirelessly visited Wrens all over the country and carried on with the work after her husband's death. The Duchess had a keen eye for fashion and dress. Always immaculate herself, she was quick to see anything wrong. On her very first appearance in uniform, she took one look at the Director WRNS, Vera Laughton Mathews, and said 'My gloves are wrong'. She was wearing white gloves, as the Navy do, but not, for some reason, the WRNS.

In 1943 the King paid two visits to the fleet at Scapa, the first in March and the second when Sir Bruce Fraser had relieved Sir John Tovey as C-in-C in August. Considering that they were wartime occasions, when little notice could be given of the King's arrival and there were very few facilities for spit and polish, they were curiously tense and formal occasions. The King himself seemed to brace himself, to wear a specially concentrated expression, when he visited his fleet.

The King arrived at Scapa in the new destroyer *Milne*. There in the vast anchorage were some famous names: Tovey's flagship *King George V*, which had taken part in the hunt for *Bismarck*; the cruiser *Scylla*, flagship of Rear Admiral R. L. Burnett, which had arrived from a Russian convoy only forty-eight hours previously and had been painted from truck to waterline in that time; officers and men had worked from dawn to dusk and the paint was barely dry; and the cruiser *Cumberland*, which by that time in the war had steamed 233,079 miles and been hit only once, at Dakar in September 1940. There were also two more battleships, *Duke of York* and *Howe*, an aircraft carrier and many more cruisers and destroyers.

The King was welcomed on board *King George V* by Sir John Tovey and in the next four days inspected ten ships in all, gave dinner parties for senior officers every night, attended divine service in the flagship on Sunday morning and an ENSA concert party by Leslie Henson and his fellow players. *Scylla* was chosen to take the King to Scrabster Pier, near Thurso. 'With all guns manned and elevated to the anti-aircraft angle, we moved through the Fleet,' wrote Lieut. Robert Hughes RNVR, *Scylla*'s Gunnery Control Officer, 'and the bugle calls floated across to us.'

'A light cruiser, less than a year in commission, was taking the Head of the Commonwealth through the ranks of his Fleet. Outside the boom the destroyer escort formed around us, the fast motor torpedo boats foamed up to their position, while overhead the Spitfire squadron roared on patrol. From the director we watched the King moving confidently about the bridge, recognising the well-known instruments, and asking about the new ones… We felt sure he was pleased to be at sea again.'

On 12th August the King was back, this time entering Scapa in the flotilla leader *Onslow*. The flagship this time was *Duke of York* and Sir Bruce Fraser, the C-in-C to welcome His Majesty. According to Midshipman Peter Cree, on watch in the flagship, 'the King was given only a short rest before his hectic rush round the fleet visiting *Shropshire* and *Tyne* before dinner, when he met the flag officers and cruiser captains.'

Cree noted in his journal that the 'complicated organisation brought into force when His Majesty is on board affects even the humble midshipmen. Bevies of gold braid are liable to shimmer over the gangway at any moment, an armed picket boat escort is required and urgent requests for boats from the Staff are even more frequent.'

On Friday 13th, the King visited two 'old ships' *Renown* and *Malaya*, the battleship *Anson*, the cruisers *London* and *Belfast*, the Greek destroyer HHMS *Themistocles*, and the Indian sloop *Godavari* (where, according to Cree, 'half the ship's company were in sick bay with nervous prostration at the thought of his visit').

The royal visits clearly were tense occasions. The King attended a concert in the fleet theatre on Sutherland Pier. Again, according to Cree, the Wren who was supposed to present His Majesty with his programme froze into immobility and had to be prodded into action from behind. There were several sketches, a Wrens' Choir, a recital of 'The Green Eye of the Little Yellow God' by two P.O.s from *Anson*, and 'Petticoat Battleship' in which the ship was supposed to be designed like dress-making ('the armoured belt — rather indelicate, only to be discussed in private').

Cree was one of those bidden to dinner. It so happened he had gone ashore weeks before on a *banyan* swimming and picnic party with the C-in-C, who had asked him to make a list of Orkney birds. When the Admiral vacated his cabin for the King, the list (of over 100 birds) happened to be left on the desk and intrigued the King. On such small chances can careers turn.

The guests were, in Cree's words, 'a motley crowd', ranging from Captains RN, to Merchant Navy captains, and commissioned warrant officers, down to midshipmen. The guests formed up in order of seniority and marched in single file aft to the Cuddy where they were all presented to His Majesty. Cree sat at a small card table with the Captain of the Fleet, the Fleet Supply Officer, and another midshipman.

The 'pleasantest touch' was flaming plum pudding served in the dark. There were 25 sixpences and the Captain of the Fleet gave Cree 'one of the two he had filched'. When only 21 sixpences had appeared, the King thought they had done badly and ordered second helpings for Cree's table.

After dinner the King showed the guests the specimen ribbons for the Africa Star and the 1939–45 Star. He had had difficulty with the design, he said, because most dyes were unobtainable in wartime. 'The evening,' Cree said, 'ended about eleven o'clock and within five minutes it seemed a dream. I never quite believed it whilst I was there, although everything was aggressively normal.'

81

Next day, the fleet weighed and, led by *Godavari*, went to sea for a day of exercises, of sub-calibre shoots, attacks by aircraft, submarines and "E-boats", and an engagement with two "enemy" cruisers. All went well, the King visited 'Y' turret (thought to be the cleanest, having a Royal Marine crew) and later came down to the gun-room for tea. 'It is most amusing,' noted Cree, mercilessly, 'watching people racking their brains for something to say.'

Commander Anthony Kimmins, the war correspondent, later described the visit in a BBC broadcast, '… when our King comes to visit his ships we feel it is just a little bit different. Just a little bit extra. You see, to us he isn't only a very distinguished visitor; he isn't only our King. He's a sailor; one of us. A man who has been through all our early Naval training, who has experienced all the hard discipline of the Naval College, who has weathered all the traditional leg-haulings and pitfalls of those first days at sea, and above all has had actual battle experience at Jutland.'

'Watch him coming down the steep ladders from the fore-bridge. There's no taking them backwards or grasping the hand-rails and cautiously picking his way down on his heels. Oh no, it's a surefooted run down with a swing off the handrail at the bottom. Countless hours as a midshipman of the watch taught him that little trick. He moves like us and he speaks our language, so do not blame us if we feel just a little — what shall I say? — possessive.'

By 1943 the Allies were rolling back the war to the enemy on almost every front. The King longed to visit his servicemen and women abroad. In June he had his wish. Travelling incognito as 'General Lyon' he flew out by RAF to Algiers on 12th for a heavy fortnight's programme. Despite long hours of travelling and the afflictions of 'Desert Tummy', the King did not spare himself. He conferred with the British and American navy and army commanders and their staffs; lunched with Giraud *and* De Gaulle; inspected troops of the 1st Army at Bone; went to Libya to inspect the 4th Indian Division, presenting Subadar Lalbahadur Thapa, of 2nd Gurkha Rifles, with his Victoria Cross.

King George V, *Howe* and two American cruisers were in Algiers harbour and Admiral Sir Andrew Cunningham 'managed to assemble a most representative parade. There were about five thousand of our own seamen and Royal Marines; some six hundred of the United States Navy, very smart and well turned-out, and, best of all, about one thousand two hundred officers and men of the Merchant Navy from the merchant vessels in the port.'

'His Majesty expressed himself as highly pleased and gratified at everything he saw. Himself a seaman, he asked many shrewd questions. He met all the British and American flag officers, and visited the American flagship and the *Howe*. Everybody was delighted to see him.'

The high point was the King's visit to Malta, the George Cross Island, which had endured a three-year siege and, even now, was not entirely free from air attack. Nobody knew better than the King himself the morale-raising effect of a personal visit.

The ship chosen to take His Majesty was the cruiser *Aurora* (Commodore W. G. Agnew) a very famous warship which, with *Penelope* and the destroyers *Lance* and *Lively*, had formed Force K — the scourge of the Axis supply routes to North Africa in 1941.

Aurora had just come back from the bombardment of Pantelleria and had only 48 hours' notice of the King's arrival, which, wrote one of her officers, 'had been preceded by tremendous exertions in the matter of scrubbing out, in a desperate attempt to look "tiddly": the bright-work on the bridge saw the light of day for the first time since the outbreak of war. Almost superhuman efforts were made to attire the ship's company in presentable suits of long whites.'

The King embarked in *Aurora* from the destroyer *Eskimo* at Tripoli on the evening of 19th June. With the escort of *Eskimo*, *Jervis*, *Nubian* and *Lookout*, *Aurora* made the 200-mile trip 'without incident', although the King passed an uncomfortable night because of rough seas and 'Desert Tummy'. At dawn a Spitfire escort roared overhead.

Sunday, 20th June, dawned bright and clear. The King stood at the salute in a special platform in front of the bridge. The Maltese people had been told of the King's arrival on the radio at 5 am and every vantage point was packed. The cheering swelled, thin at first, from a solitary Bofors crew, lined up by their gun on a harbour promontory, and growing to a tremendous crescendo as they passed *Penelope*, their old comrade-in-arms inside the harbour.

'I have witnessed many memorable spectacles,' said Admiral Cunningham, 'but this was the most impressive of them all. The dense throngs of loyal Maltese, men, women and children, were wild with enthusiasm. I have never heard such cheering, and all the bells in the many churches started ringing when he landed. Incidentally, we had no ship-sized Royal Standard, and the one flown by the *Aurora* was made and painted on board the *Howe* at Algiers.'

The King toured the bomb-shattered streets and the countryside, by car and on foot. He saw the island's G.C., presented Lord Gort the Governor with his Field Marshal's baton, and re-embarked in *Aurora* that evening, for the return trip to Tripoli. He transferred to a Motor Launch of the Free

French outside the breakwater, passed close down a line of ships all manned to cheer him, met officers and ratings of the 1st Escort Group, chatted to all the C.O.s, ordered 'Splice the Mainbrace' and signalled the Levant Escort Groups his 'high appreciation of the wonderful work done by them in bringing convoys to Malta and Tripoli'. The King flew home by RAF York transport to Northolt on 25th June, having travelled in all 6,700 miles.

In May 1944 the King visited the Home Fleet again. He was shown the midget submarines, the 'human torpedoes' in their two-man chariots. He went on board the carrier *Victorious* and watched the Barracudas and Corsairs of the Fleet Air Arm re-enact for him their attacks on the *Tirpitz* the previous month.

On 24th May 1944, the King held the least publicised and most moving of all Royal fleet reviews. He stood on steps looking over the Solent while hundreds of landing ships and landing craft of all types and sizes, the ships that were going to carry the soldiers across to France and keep them supplied, steamed past him. On 16th June, only ten days after D-Day, the King surveyed the beaches from the bridge of the cruiser *Arethusa*, and later toured the beaches in a DUKW.

The King never lost his seaman's eye. Taking passage back across the Channel in the Hunt Class destroyer *Garth*, the King thought he saw one of the escorting destroyers out of station and mentioned it to the Sub-Lieutenant RNVR on watch. The Sub checked the bearing and disagreed with the King. A little later, the King again fancied a destroyer out of station. Again, the Sub begged to differ. Eventually, his Captain took that Sub aside and spoke quietly in his ear: 'His Majesty thinks you're a bloody fool and so do I.'

In October the King visited the fleet again to say farewell to the ships which were going out to join the Eastern Fleet. He visited the army, in France, in Italy and later in the Low Countries. He took many more salutes, made many more visits and carried out many more inspections. But, in a curious way, the King's main work in the war had already been done, in those dangerous early days.

When victory came, and the King and his family waved to the crowds from the balcony of Buckingham Palace, the King could have claimed (although he would never have dreamed of doing any such thing) that he had contributed more to the war effort than any other man. He had, for example, travelled more than half a million miles in the Royal Train, which he had used as a mobile office and living rooms, and thousands more by ships and aircraft. In all his travels, he was always ready to change his arrangements and depart from precedent. On his visit to Scapa in June 1942, there was such a sea running that he had to leave in the *Morialta*, a small steamer built for coastal trading in Australia, and then used as a ratings' liberty boat. The King flew his Royal Standard (possibly the first time ever from a merchant ship) and did not forget the signal to Splice the Mainbrace, as *Morialta* steamed between the lines of warships.

After the war, the King kept up his links with the Navy, visiting ships and shore establishments whenever he could. He and the Royal Family went to South Africa in the battleship *Vanguard* in 1947. There was one incident which seemed to sum up the mutual regard of the King and the Navy. The wardroom officers had drunk His Majesty's health, in the same way that naval officers had drunk the Loyal Toast, for many years, and on many oceans. The King did not make a speech in reply. He raised his glass of port, nodded to the Mess President, and said quietly, 'Mr President, sir, your *very* good health.'

The King was to have made another trip to South Africa in *Vanguard* in 1952, but his last illness and death intervened. However, as her Captain, John Litchfield wrote years later, 'One last service the ship performed for this good, sincere and genuine man, who had been so unexpectedly called to the highest of all offices and who was to have been our shipmate, when a *Vanguard* piping party piped our beloved King "over the side" as his body left St George's Chapel at Windsor.'

HRH THE DUKE OF EDINBURGH

In July 1939, the Royal Yacht visited the Dart, and the King, the Queen, the Princesses Elizabeth and Margaret Rose, visited the Royal Naval College, where one of those who helped to entertain and look after the Royal party was Cadet HRH Prince Philip of Greece and Denmark. Princess Elizabeth and Prince Philip must have met before, at family occasions such as weddings, but this is the meeting which has attracted as much literary attention as that between Troilus and Cressida. He was eighteen and she was thirteen and it is hard to believe that anything significant happened. But after all, she was one of the most eligible young ladies, perhaps *the* most eligible, of the European Royal Families, and he certainly was one of the very few eligible young men.

Some of Prince Philip's biographers and other writers have had fun at the expense of each other on the details of that day, on whether the weather was rainy or sunny, whether the cadets had chickenpox or mumps, and how many cadets had either ailment. There was talk of the Royal party attending morning service, so it must have been a Sunday, 23rd, not 22nd, July. When the Royal Yacht, *Victoria and Albert*, or *Britannia* (*Britannia* was not, actually, launched until April 1953) steamed slowly and majestically out of Dartmouth harbour (it was Weymouth, actually, in some accounts) and the cadets rowed frantically after her in their small boats, was it not Prince Philip who was the last to give up and turn back, and were the King's precise words 'Damned young fool' or 'This is ridiculous, he must go back', or was it the 'high-pitched but commanding' voice of Lord Louis Mountbatten (who was certainly on board) which finally caused the Prince to desist?

However, as it turned out, the writers were quite correct to concentrate upon this meeting. Dartmouth was as good a place as any for a new naval member of the Royal Family to make his first publicly noticeable appearance. For here was a new kind of Royal figure. Here was somebody who did not bump along at or near the bottom of his term, thinking it in his family's tradition to pass out 67th of 68, considering himself to have done well to make 48th place. He was top man at school and top cadet, winning the King's Dirk and other prizes, at Dartmouth. He did not suffer from whooping cough, or measles, or mumps, or appendicitis, or stomach ulcers. He enjoyed excellent health. He was not seasick. He was an excellent helmsman. There was no question of his 'not going aloft' or having knock-knees. This was a runner, middle distance and long, a jumper, high and long, a thrower of javelins and cricket balls. He had no diffidence, or stammer, or speech impediment. He was a good and confident public speaker.

A certain amount of Royal woolliness had come to be expected. There was no woolliness here. This was a very able young man, difficult to beat, not at all apologetic, or careful to preserve a flawless facade. This one was never going to get his backside kicked or his ears thumped behind the squash courts. Nobody at Dartmouth was going to make him miserable, as they had made his wife-to-be's relatives miserable. If there was to be any thumping, he would be the thumper, not the thumpee. Here was one of nature's winners.

King George VI was, in a sense, the last of the old school of Royal naval officers. Prince Philip was the first of the new: perhaps the first and only. It was very fortunate for the country and the Navy that such an extremely able and adaptable man should marry the Queen. He made the perilously difficult passage from serving naval officer to consort of the Queen and remained well-respected, well thought of, both in the world he had left behind and the world he had joined. To take just one aspect, it was very healthy for the country, for the Royal Family, and for the press, to have one member of the Royal Family who was prepared to answer back. He would not suffer fools, and loved to prick the pompous, but he respected traditions. He was eager to debunk what he called 'the false, and the sham, the boaster and the fool' but, as he said, 'it is a very stupid gardener who cannot tell the difference between his weeds and his flowers.'

With his parents, Prince Andrew of Greece and Denmark and Princess Alice of Battenberg, living abroad and separated from each other, Philip himself was left on his own, and with his own living to make. He was influenced by his two naval uncles, George, 2nd Marquess of Milford Haven, and after his death in 1938, Lord Louis Mountbatten. The Navy seemed a natural choice, but it was not by any means cut and dried. His uncles must have stressed its advantages, painted as rosy a picture as they could, pointed out that it would be possible to get a commission. Left to himself, as he once said, Prince Philip would have 'gone into the Air Force, without a doubt'.

In the end, the Navy won, and Prince Philip went to Dartmouth in May 1939 as a Special Entry cadet, under a scheme whereby boys joined at 17 or 18 years old, having already had their education at a normal school, rather than joining at 12 or 13 years old and having their general education at Dartmouth.

Prince Philip passed out top, and was promoted Midshipman on 1st January 1940. He was still a Greek citizen (born on the island of Corfu, on 10th June 1921) and for the first year of the war was a neutral although serving in the Royal Navy. His uncle, Lord Louis, warned him there might be problems about his naturalisation and the first moves were made. But bureaucracy moved even more slowly in wartime and in fact Prince Philip was not naturalised as a British citizen until 28th February 1947.

The Foreign Office was anxious that a neutral Greek Royal prince should be kept away from the warzone, (presumably in case of embarrassment if he should be killed or, with others, be responsible for killing somebody else) and Prince Philip's first ship was the veteran battleship *Ramillies*, then largely engaged in escorting troop convoys across the Indian Ocean from Australia and New Zealand to Alexandria.

Prince Philip joined her on 20th February 1940, to live with another eighteen midshipmen in a hot, poorly ventilated, overcrowded, cockroach-ridden gunroom, which smelt (as all gunrooms always do) of beer, where nobody ever turned in to their hammocks but crashed out where they could on armchairs, sofas and settees. Prince Philip kept watches, took sunsights, made cocoa, listened to tall stories from the lookouts, just as all midshipmen do. His special duty was Captain's Doggie, his function being to trail behind the great man, run errands, carry messages, and generally bask vicariously in reflected glory.

All midshipmen had to keep a Journal, which was a large format bound book specially provided by Their Lordships, in which midshipmen were to write, in their own words, a daily account of events of interest and importance in their ship, their fleet, or on the international scene. A Journal helped a midshipman to train his powers of observation and expression, and inculcated the habit of orderliness. Journals were inspected once a week by the "Snotties' Nurse" on board (the officer, normally a senior Lieutenant Commander, nominated to supervise midshipmen's training) and by the Captain probably once a month and certainly once a quarter.

Luckily, Prince Philip's Journal still survives. First-hand, eyewitness accounts of the war at sea, from the point of view of a junior officer, are very rare indeed and so the Journal has tremendous historical interest, quite apart from any royal connotations. Equally fortunately, the Journal was made available to Prince Philip's 'informal' biographer, Basil Boothroyd, for a book published to coincide with its subject's 50th birthday. It gives a clear account of Prince Philip's life in 1940–41.

It also shows how he was moved from ship to ship, to avoid the least chance of being involved in hostilities. When he joined the cruiser *Shropshire* on 1st October 1940, he noted sardonically in his Journal that she was 'the third ship in eight months to receive this singular honour'. On 12th April, when *Ramillies* was on her way to Alexandria, Prince Philip had left her to join the 'County' Class cruiser *Kent*, flagship of the C-in-C China Station.

The 'County' Class, like *Kent* and *Shropshire*, were the nearest the Navy ever got to 'gentlemen's conveyances'. They were big — 10,000 tons — and fast — 31 knots — and spacious, with lots of headroom, three funnels (which the sailors always said were to impress the Chinese) and heavily armed, with eight 8-inch, in double turrets. *Kent* had already spent a full commission in the Far East and, but for the war, would have gone home to pay off.

The news that a Prince with royal connections was joining was received with a certain amount of messdeck tooth-sucking. 'We'd already got a banack routine, matchstick sentries, a change of rig five or six times a day, and an Admiral on the quarterdeck. Now we had to have Royalty.'

But *Kent*'s sailors discovered, as sailors had before and were to discover again, that the royal midshipmen asked no favours, expected no special discounts, put on no special airs, but tried to do their job as best they could. 'I can honestly say that when we first saw this gangling youth, running all over the ship trying to obey instructions from a host of gold braid, smiling and cheerful to everyone, no matter what their rank, he immediately became endeared to us'. The Captain thought he was 'my best midshipman' and the ship's company would certainly have agreed with Leading Signalman William Beattie, that 'we were sorry when he left us.'

When Prince Philip left *Shropshire* at Durban in December 1940 he was no longer a neutral. On 28th October Italy had invaded Greece. His next ship was another battleship, *Valiant*, also like *Ramillies* dating from the First World War, but recently refitted, modernised and equipped with surface radar sets. In her Prince Philip was soon in action, at the bombardment of Bardia on the Libyan coast, on 2nd January 1942. The Journal gives a terse but evocative account '... We arrived off the coast on Thursday morning at dawn. In the dark the flashes of the guns could be seen a long way out to sea... The whole operation was a very spectacular affair...'

An even more spectacular affair followed on 10th January, when *Valiant* was at sea with the fleet, which included the carrier *Illustrious*, as support force for a convoy westbound for Malta and, ultimately, Piraeus. The activity began very early in the day, according to the Journal '... at dawn action stations on Friday gun flashes were sighted on the starboard bow. We increased speed to investigate, and by the time we were within five miles it was almost daylight. *Bonaventure* signalled that

Southampton and herself were engaging two enemy destroyers. We could just see one of the destroyers blowing up in a cloud of smoke and spray. The other escaped. Shortly after this the destroyer *Gallant* hit a mine and her bow was blown off, and floated slowly away on the swell...'

Shortly after midday, two Savoia-Marchetti S.79 torpedo bombers attacked *Valiant* 'but a quick alteration of course foiled their attempt, and their fish passed down the port side.' The fleet was still about 100 miles west of Malta, with the convoy and escort to the southward. *Illustrious'* Fulmar fighters pursued *Valiant's* attackers but, while they were away so engaged, a force of some forty to fifty Ju.87 and Ju.88 bombers arrived overhead. *Illustrious* flew off more Fulmars but they were unable to gain height before the enemy fell upon their ship.

This was almost the first occasion the Luftwaffe had been seen at sea in the Mediterranean. General Geissler's Fliegerkorps X, who had specially trained for attacks on ships, had recently arrived and deployed to airfields in Sicily and in southern Italy. From the first attack it was quite clear to the Mediterranean Fleet that here was a new foe in the field. The high-level bombing of the Italian Regio Aeronautica had been by no means negligible, but this was something quite new.

Even Cunningham, the C-in-C, was impressed. '... There was no doubt we were watching complete experts... We could not but admire the skill and precision of it all...' he wrote. 'The attacks were pressed home to point-blank range...'

Illustrious was the main target. She suffered six hits from 500kg bombs in ten minutes. But for her armoured flight deck, she must have been lost. But she survived, very badly damaged and on fire, and reached Malta that evening. Meanwhile the dive-bombers concentrated on *Valiant* 'and five bombs dropped fairly close. A number of splinters fell on the ship but there were no casualties. A terrific barrage was put up by the fleet, but it did not seem to have any effect on these artificially [*sic*] courageous men.'

Later in the afternoon, *Valiant* 'received another dose from the dive-bombers. Fourteen this time concentrated on us. All their bombs fell very close and most of their attacks were delivered from right astern. Bomb splinters and machine gun bullets sprayed along the length of the upper deck.' *Valiant* suffered minor damage to her superstructure and some underwater damage but she was present at the next action, off Cape Matapan.

In March 1941 the Mediterranean Fleet was fully occupied in escorting troop reinforcements and supply convoys for the campaign in Greece. Towards the end of the month, the Italian Navy at last responded to tremendous pressure from the Germans to make some attempt to interfere with the convoys by surface ship action. Fortunately for the Allies, the Italian plans were also communicated to the Luftwaffe, whose codes had been penetrated. Details of the Italian plans became known to Cunningham and his staff.

By 27th March, it was known that an Italian fleet, including the battleship *Vittorio Veneto*, was at sea. The Mediterranean Fleet sailed that evening, with three battleships, *Warspite* (flying Cunningham's flag), *Valiant* and *Barham*, the aircraft carrier *Formidable*, a cruiser force under Vice Admiral Pridham-Wippell, and accompanying destroyers.

Next day, 28th March, Pridham-Wippell's cruisers were in action with the enemy and aircraft from *Formidable* scored a torpedo hit on *Vittorio Veneto*, and also on the heavy cruiser *Pola*, crippling her and bringing her to a dead stop in the water. That evening, when darkness had fallen, first Pridham-

Wippell's cruisers, and then *Valiant*'s radar reported a contact on their screens: a large unknown ship lying, apparently stopped, to port of the battle fleet.

Cunningham gleefully urged his ships onwards through the night. This contact could well be *Vittorio Veneto*, just waiting for the *coup de grâce*. Cunningham had trained his ships to fight at night. Now, the first night action of the war, and the first radar-assisted naval action in history, was about to begin.

The Italian Admiral Iachino had not been nearly so well served by air reconnaissance during the day as his opponent. At nightfall he had no idea Cunningham's ships were as close as they actually were. Confidently, he detached the two heavy cruisers *Fiume* and *Zara* to assist the stricken *Pola*. At 10.25 Cunningham's ships were so close that these three cruisers were actually seen and identified from *Warspite*'s bridge.

Guided by radar, Cunningham's battleships closed to what was, for their 15-inch guns, point-blank range: 3,800 yards. The searchlights shone out, the great guns opened fire, and the first salvoes were on their way.

The Italian cruisers were caught utterly unaware, with their gun turrets still trained fore and aft. Five of *Warspite*'s first salvo of six hit and she went on hitting. The Italian ships were smashed into helpless ruins before they could make any reply. In Cunningham's words, it was 'a ghastly sight.'

Valiant, astern of *Warspite*, opened fire at the same time and Cunningham turned to watch her 'pounding her ship to bits. Her rapidity of fire astonished me. Never would I have believed it possible with these heavy guns.' It was not a fight but a massacre. Prince Philip himself said it was 'as near murder as anything could be in wartime. The cruisers just burst into tremendous sheets of flame.'

Prince Philip was in charge of *Valiant*'s searchlight battery. The Journal gives an excellent tactual account of his view: 'My orders were that if any ship illuminated a target I was to switch on and illuminate it for the rest of the fleet, so when this ship was lit up by a rather dim light from what I thought was the flagship I switched on our midship light which picked out the enemy cruiser and lit her up as if it were broad daylight. She was only seen complete in the light for a few seconds as the flagship had already opened fire, and as her first broadside landed and hit she was blotted out from just abaft the bridge to right astern. We fired our first broadside about 7 seconds after the flagship with very much the same effect. The broadside only consisted of "A" and "B" turrets as the after turrets would not bear.

'By now all the secondary armament of both ships had opened fire and the noise was considerable. The Captain and the Gunnery Officer now began shouting from the bridge for the searchlights to train left. The idea that there might have been another ship, with the one we were firing at, never entered my head, so it was some few moments before I was persuaded to relinquish the blazing target and search for another one I had no reason to believe was there. However, training to the left, the light picked up another cruiser, ahead of the first one by some 3 or 4 cables. As the enemy was so close the light did not illuminate the whole ship but only about ¾ of it, so I trained left over the whole ship until the bridge structure was in the centre of the beam. The effect was rather like flashing a strong torch on a small model about 5 yards away… She was illuminated in an undamaged condition for the period of about 5 seconds when our second broadside left the ship, and almost at once she was completely blotted out from stem to stern…

'When that broadside was fired, owing to the noise of the secondary armament, I did not hear the "ting-ting" from the DCT, the result was that the glasses were rammed into my eyes, and flash almost blinded me. Luckily the searchlight was not affected so that when I was able to see something again the light was still on target. Four more broadsides were fired at the enemy, and more than 70% of the shells must have hit. The only correction given by the control officer was "left 1°"', as he thought we were hitting a bit far aft.

'When the enemy had completely vanished in clouds of smoke and steam we ceased firing and switched the light off.' As it turned out, all three Italian cruisers, and one destroyer, *Altieri*, were sunk that night. It was a tremendous victory for the Mediterranean Fleet and a terrific boost for national morale, at a time when morale badly needed encouragement.

After repairing most of her bomb and splinter damage, *Valiant* once more escorted troop convoys, to Greece and then Crete. German paratroopers landed in Crete on 20th May 1941, and a short, sharp but vicious battle for the island began. At sea, Cunningham's ships endured a prolonged ordeal by air attack. The Journal recorded in excellent war-reporting style, some stirring events: 'Next day (21st May) things began to get worse. *Juno* was sunk. *Naiad* and *Carlisle* were hit. A signal came asking for assistance so we turned and steamed at 20 knots… As we came in sight of the Straits we saw *Naiad* and *Carlisle* being attacked by bombers. We went straight in to within 10 miles of Crete and then the bombing started in earnest. Stukas came over but avoided the big ships and went for the crippled cruisers and destroyer screens.'

On 22nd May, '*Greyhound* was hit right aft by a large bomb, her stern blew up and she sank about twenty minutes later.' The cruisers *Gloucester* and *Fiji* were sent in to help but they too were sunk. 'Three Me. 109s attacked *Warspite* as dive-bombers, and she was hit just where her starboard forrard mounting was…' The fleet then had some more attention, and we were bombed from a high level by a number of small bombs dropped in sticks of 12 or more. One Dornier came straight for us from the port beam and dropped 12 bombs when he was almost overhead. We turned to port and ceased firing, when suddenly the bombs came whistling down, landing very close all down the port side.'

'It was only some time later that I discovered we had been hit twice on the quarterdeck.' One bomb exploded just aft of the quarterdeck screen, port side, the other within twenty feet, just inboard of the quarterdeck guardrails, 'blowing a hole into the wardroom laundry'. There were four casualties.

The 22nd and 23rd May 1941 were two of the hardest days in the Navy's history. Early on 23rd, the 5th Destroyer Flotilla, whose Captain (D) was Lord Louis Mountbatten, was caught in the open near to the Crete coast by Ju.87s and Ju.88s. *Kashmir* was hit first, and then *Kelly*. She was turning under full helm at 30 knots when she was hit and her Captain saw she was 'rolling right over, I suddenly saw the water rise on our port side in a raging torrent of over thirty knots and thinking, "Whatever happens I must stay with the ship as long as I can. I must be the last to leave her alive". We were over beyond ninety degrees now… With my arms I clung round the gyro compass pedestal. And then the sea came in a roaring maelstrom. I saw officers and men struggling to get out of the bridge and then took an enormously deep breath as the water closed over my head… I suddenly felt my lungs were going to burst and that I would have to open my mouth unless I could somehow keep it shut. With my right hand I gripped my mouth in a vice-like grip and with my left I held my nostrils shut. It was a fight of willpower… Slowly, infinitely slowly, the water got brighter and lighter and then suddenly with lungs bursting I broke surface…'

Survivors from *Kelly* and *Kashmir* were taken to Alexandria in *Kipling*, and cheered by every ship in harbour. 'At the landing stage,' wrote Captain (D), 'I was met by the cheery, grinning face of our nephew Philip who had come to meet me. He roared with laughter on seeing me and when I asked him what was up he said "You have no idea how funny you look." I had forgotten how completely smothered we all were in oil fuel.'

By 28th May the struggle for Crete was coming to an end and the army had to be evacuated. This involved tremendous risk for the ships. Cunningham disliked 'yes men' on his staff, and when his staff pointed out the dangers, as it was their duty to do, Cunningham said: 'The army *must* be taken off. It takes the Navy three years to build a ship. It would take three hundred to rebuild a tradition.'

So began another ordeal which reached its climax on 29th May when the cruisers *Perth* and *Dido* were damaged, and the destroyers *Imperial* and *Hereward* were sunk. The cruiser *Orion* was machine-gunned. Captain Back was killed on his bridge and Rear Admiral Bernard Rawlings was wounded. There was worse to come. A bomb exploded in a messdeck packed with exhausted soldiers. Prince Philip's Journal recorded that '*Orion* was hit by two bombs. One of them completely wrecked "A" turret, the other went in through the bridge, down five decks and exploded making an enormous hole killing 140 sailors, and 200 soldiers who were being evacuated.'

On 1st June the cruiser *Calcutta* was sunk. *Formidable* was attacked and badly damaged. 'For almost a week this went on day after day, ships coming in packed with troops, destroyers showing not-under-control balls, cruisers peppered with shrapnel from near-misses…' But it was worth it in the end. The army was taken off. One New Zealander wrote that when they reached the coast 'With a torch we flashed an S.O.S. and, to our tremendous relief, we received an answer. It was the Navy on the job — the Navy for which we had been hoping and praying all along the route.'

For his part at Matapan, Prince Philip was mentioned in the dispatches of Captain Charles Morgan, commanding *Valiant*. It was noted on the form of recommendation that he already had the Grand Cross of the Order of the Redeemer (Greek), the Medal (4th Class) of the Order of St Constantine and St George (Greek), and the Coronation Medal. The citation said: 'Was searchlight midshipman during the Battle of Cape Matapan. The successful and continuous illumination of the enemy greatly contributed to the devastating results achieved in the gun action.' This was endorsed in due course by Pridham-Wippell, then commanding 1st Battle Squadron and, in September 1941, by Cunningham the C-in-C. King George of Greece, who had been himself one of the last to be evacuated, in the destroyer *Decoy*, later awarded him the Greek Cross of Valour.

Prince Philip's Journal stops abruptly at the end of May, when he went home to do his sub-lieutenant's courses. Going home in mid-1941 meant going round the Cape of Good Hope, and hitching one's passage on any troopship or warship that happened to be going in the right direction. Prince Philip sailed with four other midshipmen in the liner *Duchess of Atholl*, then doing trooping duties, as far as Durban, where they transferred to another troopship bound for U.K. via Halifax, Nova Scotia, to embark Canadian troops. For very junior officers, going home could also mean working one's passage: the ship got as far as Puerto Rico, where the lascar stokers mutinied and then deserted. The five midshipmen were told they had volunteered as relief firemen, and stoked the boilers for six days, as far as Halifax.

Many years later, when he had become an Admiral of the Fleet and was presenting the prizes to the cadets in the training cruiser *Devonshire*, Prince Philip said he was quite familiar with the experience of those who had not won prizes, and they had his sympathy. This was a disarming way of opening a speech but it was not true. He had already won prizes at Dartmouth and in his subs courses in gunnery, navigation, torpedo and anti-submarine, damage control, and a Greenwich course in general studies and naval history, which he started in September 1941, Prince Philip gained four first-class passes and one second. These results gave him nine months accelerated and back-dated promotion to the rank of Sub-Lieutenant in February 1941. He joined his first ship as a commissioned officer on 28th January 1942, at Sheerness.

She was HMS *Wallace*, *a* somewhat elderly destroyer launched in 1918 as a flotilla leader for the famous 'V' and 'W' Class destroyers. In 1939 she had been converted as an anti-aircraft escort, known as a 'WAIR'; her torpedo tubes were removed, and her 4.7 guns replaced by two twin 4-inch high-angle gun mountings fore and aft. She had a nominal complement of 183 but in wartime she was overcrowded and overworked, like all destroyers.

The flotilla commander was Commander J. M. Rowland DSO, a famous figure from the Battle of the Atlantic, who in command of *Wolverine* in March 1941 sank U-47 with all hands, including Prien. *Wallace*'s captain was Lt. Cdr. E. G. Heywood-Lonsdale, her First Lieutenant E. F. Hamilton-Meikle. The wardroom also included a Lieutenant RNVR, two temporary

Sub. Lts. RNVR the Commissioned Engineer, the Gunner and a Surgeon Lt. RNVR.

Wallace was then based at Rosyth, as leader of the Rosyth Escort Force, and one of the regular escorts for the East coast convoys, from the Firth of Forth to Sheerness, down through what was known as 'E-boat alley'. It was a hazardous operational area. 'Convoys ran like trains,' wrote Leading Telegraphist Michael Joyce, one of *Wallace*'s ship's company, 'one left Methil for the south every day and another from Sheerness for the north, throughout the whole war. Under normal conditions, the trip took 2½ days in each direction with about 12 hours at Sheerness and possibly 24 hours in Rosyth.

'In the narrow confines of the East Coast — bounded to seaward by our own mine barrier — there was no room for evasive action when enemy attacks occurred. In the early days, convoys could be made up to over 100 merchant vessels, and from the Wash southwards you were in single file which resulted in a convoy that could be over 20 miles in length from front to rear. Attacks by aircraft and E-boats were commonplace and when mines and the treacherous weather of the North Sea were added, the demands made on destroyers escorting convoys were high.'

On 1st April, ten Norwegian ships broke out of the Swedish port of Gothenburg, making for Britain. Six destroyers, including *Wallace*, were sent to meet them. But in the meantime the Luftwaffe had found and attacked them. Five ships were sunk, scuttled or grounded, and two returned to Gothenburg. *Wallace*, in the account of Ordinary Seaman Eric Oates, 'came across another one being attacked by German bombers. This one we had to sink after attempting to fight off the attackers.' Only two ships reached England.

Oates describes one day when '*Wallace* was in collision after leaving Sheerness in a thick fog whilst taking evasive action from a bomber flying overhead. A merchant ship leading one line of the convoy cut right into the forward boiler room, killing a leading stoker and badly scalding two others. I did not see this myself but I was told that Prince Philip went down into the flooded boiler-room to try and free the trapped men. The *Wallace* was then unable to make steam and we had to wait a long time for a sea-going tug to tow us into Sheerness.'

The ship's company had had mixed feelings about a Royal prince joining them. According to Oates, 'I remember it created a seven day wonder...' But Joyce took a cooler view: 'The peace-time Navy was well-sprinkled with titles. Earls, Dukes, Baronets and Honourables were plentiful, and at that time — nobody had ever heard of Prince Philip of Greece and Denmark!'

'Officers in the Navy,' Joyce wrote, 'were known as either "Toffs" or "Pigs" (and probably still are) — and there was no intermediate category. A Toff was one who knew his job and did it well, and who also was approachable and paid regard to the men of the Lower Deck. "Pigs" were the opposite. It did not take long for Prince Philip to prove that he was a "Toff" — a title not easily earned. He was keen and demanded the highest efficiency from all. He did not suffer fools gladly, and could display a very sharp tongue with those who fell short of his standards.'

Prince Philip was promoted Lieutenant on 16th July 1942 and when Hamilton-Meikle left the ship he became First Lieutenant. There were always those ready to whisper that Prince Philip's promotion was due to string-pulling by his uncle Lord Louis Mountbatten. This was a slander, on both men.

At that time Prince Philip had the enormous advantage of being able to live a normal life, free from publicity, and move about as freely as any other private citizen. As Joyce wrote, putting his finger on a real point, 'in the Rosyth, Dunfermline and Edinburgh areas, naval officers were "two a penny", and Prince Philip was just another one. He was completely unknown and therefore could indulge in normal pursuits. He could mix with the public; go to the cinema; drink a pint in a pub, and nobody took any notice. I recall a Ship's Dance in Dunfermline when he threw himself into the spirit of things — dancing eightsome reels etc., and the local ladies who had provided the refreshments were amazed and flustered when they learned they had danced with a real, live Prince!'

Years later, when he was receiving the Freedom of Edinburgh, Prince Philip recalled those days and paid the city a graceful compliment. 'I was based at Rosyth for nearly two years,' he said, 'and I know that whenever we had the chance we used to jump into the train at Inverkeithing and come here. I know we were a dreadful nuisance and frequently misbehaved, but as a result of your forbearance we all have a very tender spot for the "Burg"… You in this city did a great deal for servicemen, not because you *had* to but because you knew it would be kind and right…'

By 1943 the East Coast convoy escorts had fought and largely won the battle against the enemy. Our own effort became less defensive and turned more to the attack of German shipping. So it was in a comparative lull at home that *Wallace* steamed down to the Mediterranean to take part in the Allied invasion of Sicily, Operation HUSKY, in July 1943. Her captain was Lieutenant Duncan Carson, who had taken command on 18th May 1943, with Prince Philip still as Number One.

HUSKY was the largest amphibious landing of the war, a vast and complex operation involving hundreds of ships and many thousands of men. *Wallace* was part of the British Eastern Naval Task Force under Admiral Sir Bertram Ramsay, in Force V, commanded by Admiral Vian. Her specific task was to cover the landings of 1st Canadian Division in Sector Bark West, on the southeastern tip of Sicily.

The night after the landing was clear, with bright moonlight, and the Luftwaffe, flying from southern Italy, several times attacked shipping lying off the beaches. Oates recalls that 'on the second night we were subjected to a prolonged dive bombing by Stukas and were continually at action stations.' *Wallace* 'carried out patrols off Sicily after the initial landings,' wrote Joyce. 'On one occasion she was attacked by enemy aircraft for over 2½ hours without any help being given or expected, and Prince Philip coolly directed most of the operations from the bridge.'

Wallace returned to the United Kingdom in September, escorted East coast convoys again until November, when she was paid off into refit. Prince Philip spent some of his leave at Windsor Castle. In February 1944 Prince Philip travelled up to Hebburn on Tyne, to join the destroyer *Whelp*, building at Hawthorn Leslie's. He joined on 14th and his Captain, Commander George A. F. Norfolk, joined a fortnight later.

Soon after he arrived he gave his first newspaper interview — to Miss Olga Franklin, then a reporter on the *Newcastle Journal*, later to become a very well-known Fleet Street personality, with her own column 'Frankly Yours' on the *Daily Mail*.

Whatever preconceived ideas Miss Franklin might have had about swarthy Greek types, she was much struck by the reality. Under the headline 'Shipyard Stranger Is a Royal Prince', she wrote 'Very few workers in a North-East shipyard are aware that the tall, ash-blond first lieutenant, RN, who travels by bus to work among them each day, is a Royal Prince.'

Citizens have been equally unaware that this 23-year-old naval officer, Prince Philip of Greece, has been living quietly in an hotel while 'standing by' on a British destroyer.

Prince Philip, who has the looks of a typical Prince of a Hans Andersen fairy tale, will certainly have been noticed by many a girl worker at the shipyard.

I found that his Scandinavian appearance is explained by the fact that his grandfather, King George I of the Hellenes, was the son of King Christian IX of Denmark, and was nominated for the Greek Throne by the British government at the request of the Greek National Assembly in 1862.

Prince Philip, who has served with the British Mediterranean Fleet, and wears the 1939–43 Africa Star [*sic*], is the only son of Prince Andrew, fourth child [sic: actually seventh child, fourth son] of George I of Greece and Princess Alice.

The Prince was amused at my suggestion that he might find the northern dialect difficult to understand.

'I understand the local people perfectly,' he said, 'and I am enjoying my stay.'

This was confirmed by another naval officer.

The Prince said: 'I last saw my home in Athens in February 1941.' He added that he had been in England twice before — to school.

This is the first time the Prince has been interviewed and reported in this country … and I thanked him for the good humoured and kindly way he had accepted 'exposure'.

First Lieutenant of a destroyer is one of the best jobs in the Navy — to be captain of a destroyer is the only better one. Number One is *ex officio* President of the wardroom mess, senior bridge watch-keeper, responsible to the Captain for the ship's fighting efficiency, cleanliness, discipline, routine, morale, recreation, food, sailors' welfare and living conditions.

Chief Petty Officer W. A. Magill was Torpedo Coxswain of *Whelp* for the last eighteen months of her commission, met and discussed ship's affairs with Prince Philip daily, and as the Coxswain is traditionally a destroyer's regulating officer, and Hon. Sec. of the Canteen Committee, his right-hand man. Of his First Lieutenant, Magill wrote: 'As an officer he was very efficient and tried to know as much as he could about all the various departments' jobs and would take part with repairs etc.; nothing took place on board without his participation.'

By now, the Navy, if not the press at home, had the first scent of a possible royal romance. 'It was generally known on board ship he was "courting" the Princess as their letters going and coming were as informal as our own. The Princess's envelopes bore no special mark and The Duke took no umbrage (if that's the right word) if the lads shouted out, "There's Jimmy's party" when the Princess was seen on the makeshift cinema screen we saw Pathé News on occasionally when we were in harbour'.

Whelp commissioned in the spring of 1944 and went to Scapa Flow for work-up and exercises. In August she sailed for the Far East (having been present during the King's visit to the Home Fleet that summer) via Gibraltar, Malta, Alexandria, Port Said, Suez, and finally Trincomalee, the great fleet base and harbour in Ceylon (Sri Lanka).

At Trinco, *Whelp* joined the 27th Destroyer Flotilla of *Kempenfelt* (Captain [D]), *Wakeful*, *Whirlwind*, *Wager*, *Wessex* and *Whelp*. First Lieutenant of *Whelp*'s 'chummy ship' *Wessex* was Lieutenant J. M. A. ('Mike') Parker, an Australian who had joined the Royal Navy before the war. He had also been First

Lieutenant of the 'next door' destroyer *Lauderdale* when Prince Philip had been in *Wallace*. He became one of Prince Philip's closest friends, and, later, his equerry.

With the 27th D.F., *Whelp* joined in the daily round and common task of a destroyer flotilla, with the occasional excitement. On 7th January 1945 she met the submarine *Shakespeare* at sea and towed her back alongside the depot ship *Wolfe*. *Shakespeare* had had a remarkable escape: bombed by Japanese aircraft off the Andaman Islands, she had suffered casualties and damage including a hole in her pressure hull, preventing her diving, but she had escaped on the surface.

Whelp was part of the destroyer escort for the British Pacific Fleet's strike at the oil refineries at Pangkalan Brandan in Sumatra on 4th January and again for two much larger strikes, in which over 100 aircraft from four carriers took part, on refineries and storage tanks at Palembang near the east coast of Sumatra on 24th and 29th January. The giant refineries were put out of action for some months and never regained full production for the rest of the war. *Whelp* then sailed for Australia with the fleet.

The Pacific war which the British Pacific Fleet now expected to join was a colossal oceanic struggle, fought over thousands of miles and involving carrier forces which were quite unknown in the European and Atlantic theatres. A small parcel of four carriers, such as the British had, made up only one group in a task force (although the U.S. Navy courteously designated the BPF a task force). The fleet sailed from Sydney in February 1945, only to endure a most unpleasant period of suspense at the great anchorage of Manus in the Admiralty Islands, when it seemed that it would not be allowed to take part in the campaign in Okinawa after all.

At last, in March, the fleet sailed. Its task was necessary but unglamorous: to bomb the runways on the Sakishima Islands which ran like a chain from Formosa to Okinawa, and prevent the Japanese staging replacement aircraft through them. It was a weary task, because the Japanese industriously filled in the bomb craters every night.

It was also extremely dangerous. Lacking a fleet, the Japanese retaliated with clouds of Kamikaze suicide aircraft. The destroyer *Ulster* was hit and so badly damaged she was towed away. All five of the British carriers who took part were hit by kamikazes at one time or another. They were saved by their armoured decks (her flight deck saved *Illustrious* in 1945, just as it had in 1941).

For destroyers it was a busy life, constantly changing position in the fleet or on the screen, taking up new stations for night cruising, air defence, radar picket, and replenishment at sea. It was, as the C-in-C, Admiral Sir Bruce Fraser said, 'an intensive, efficient and hard striking type of war ... and nothing but the best would be tolerated.'

On 23rd April the fleet arrived at Leyte in the Philippines for a replenishment and repair period, after which *Illustrious*, the cruiser *Argonaut*, and *Whelp* and *Wager* returned to Sydney for refit (and *Illustrious*, eventually, for home). On 6th August *Whelp* sailed again with *Wager* to escort Admiral Fraser's flagship the battleship *Duke of York* to Guam where Admiral Chester Nimitz, Supreme Allied Commander Pacific Area, had his headquarters. There, Fraser invested Nimitz as Knight Grand Cross of the Order of the Bath (GCB) before sailing on 13th to join the BPF at sea.

The atomic bombs had already been dropped and the war was clearly almost over, when *Duke of York* and her destroyers joined the American Third Fleet at dawn on 16th August, at sea some 200 miles south-east of Tokyo. Fraser transferred to the fleet commander Admiral Halsey's flagship, the battleship *Missouri*, and invested him as Knight Commander of the Order of the British Empire (KBE), very probably the only occasion when such an Order has been bestowed upon a foreign admiral on board his flagship by a British C-in-C.

Shortage of oil fuel forced the greater part of the BPF, to its intense disappointment, to leave before the end. But *Whelp* and *Wager* escorted *Duke of York* into Tokyo Bay for the signing of the Japanese surrender, which took place on board *Missouri* on 2nd September. 'The silence was complete,' wrote Fraser, who signed for the United Kingdom, 'except for the whirring and clicking of cameras, and one could feel that all present at the gathering were struggling to adjust themselves mentally to the fact that they were witnessing the act which put an end to a long and bitter war.'

Whelp with other destroyers took part in the repatriation of Allied POWs, then sailed home, arriving in Portsmouth in January 1946. Prince Philip was in temporary command for two months before leaving. He had had as active and as violent a war as any man. He had served in battleships, cruisers and destroyers. He had experience of a large amphibious landing, and he had served in the long-ranging, fast-moving Pacific war, when fleets put to sea for months, being supplied by a Fleet Train of tankers and supply ships. (He had not served in carriers, and had no experience of flying, but he would put that right in time.) But now, suddenly, it was all over. He was able to pay some attention at last to his private life.

His first post-war appointment was to a shore establishment HMS *Glendower*, which had been a holiday camp before the war, at Pwllheli, in North Wales. But he had only been there a few weeks when it closed down, being returned to Butlin's, its pre-war owners.

His next appointment was an interesting and an important one: course officer at HMS *Royal Arthur*, then largely a collection of Nissen huts on a windy Wiltshire hillside but eventually to become the Petty Officer's School. Prince Philip was one of two officers who arranged and carried out the course, giving the lectures, setting the problems, and grading the personalities who passed through. Some two hundred newly-rated petty officers at a time underwent the course in leadership, current affairs, with some naval history, designed to encourage their initiative, broaden their outlooks, boost their self-confidence, and improve themselves as leaders of men. It was good for the Navy and good for the young men themselves that petty officers of different specialisations all took the same course, mixed together, exchanged views and endured the same rigours (it was, apart from everything else, an extremely cold winter).

It was very probably in the summer of 1946 and at Balmoral that Prince Philip proposed to Princess Elizabeth (or perhaps it was the royal privilege for the young lady to ask the question). There had been increasing speculation about the ninety-mile dashes in his little black MG motor car from Wiltshire to London, the appearances at the side entrance to Buckingham Palace, Christmas 1946 spent at Sandringham, tell-tale references to 'Philip' in the Princess's own conversation. All speculation ended when the Royal Family returned from their trip to South Africa in *Vanguard* and the Royal engagement was announced on 10th July 1947. Prince Philip had not only become a naturalised British citizen but had taken the surname Mountbatten.

On 19th November 1947, the eve of his wedding at Westminster Abbey, Prince Philip was made a Knight of the Garter, Baron Greenwich, Earl of Merioneth and Duke of Edinburgh (the last title a neat look-back to 'Affie', Victoria's second son, and the man who had encouraged Philip's great-uncle Prince Louis of Battenberg to join the Navy). There was a strong naval representation at the 'stag' bachelor party that evening: 'Gaffer' Norfolk, Mike Parker, David Milford Haven (who was best man) and Lord Louis Mountbatten among others.

After his wedding, the Duke of Edinburgh no longer had any chance of continuing a normal naval career. It was a great loss to him, and to the Navy. The Navy had been his life. He was good at it. He was a most able officer. Clement Attlee, a good and shrewd judge of men, thought he might have risen as high in the Navy as his uncle Lord Mountbatten. He still had much to contribute to the Service, but it would not be as a serving officer. The Royal Family themselves were well aware of how much the Duke was giving up.

But his career still had some years to run, and in the meantime the couple lived at Clarence House and, every morning, the Duke walked across the park to his first job as a married man, in the Operations Division of the Admiralty. He was, he said, 'just a dogsbody. Shuffling ships around. It was quite interesting.' In April 1948 the Duke went to Greenwich for a three-month staff course, studying naval history, strategy, civics and economic history. The 'students', normally officers up to the rank of Commander, made appreciations of situations, played out tactical exercises, prepared lectures for each other, criticised each other's performances. It was in a way, the nearest the Navy came to a University course.

Commander David Bird, then a Lieutenant on the same course with 'the next desk in the same syndicate', noted that the Duke 'did the whole course with no holds barred despite his many other duties, in fact we gathered that Princess Elizabeth, as she then was, did most of the course, too, once removed, so to speak, as she used to help him like other wives did with his appreciations and other written work.'

'He used to give three of us a lift to Waterloo to catch our week-end train on Fridays. On one occasion when we were not due back until Tuesday, as Monday was Whit-Monday, he said "It's all right for you but I've got to go to France and make three speeches in French". When he turned up on Tuesday he was hopping mad. He had had two sacks of mail complaining that they had gone to the races at Chantilly on Sunday. He said it was the only break they had, and "We'd been to church in the morning and I bet a lot of them hadn't."'

The anecdote is a most revealing example of the pressures of trying to combine careers, in the Navy, and as a working member of the Royal Family. The Duke was rightly incensed by the criticism (one self-righteous clergyman even described that Sunday as "a dark day in our history"!).

On 14th November 1948, the Duke became a father. The Navy spliced the mainbrace and called down blessings upon the infant Charles' innocent head. Meanwhile, Royal engagements, visits, functions, honorary posts and offices, poured down on his father's head. But on 17th October 1949 the Duke was appointed First Lieutenant of the destroyer HMS *Chequers*, leader of the 1st Flotilla in Malta, with a four-ring Captain, Michael Townsend, DSO, OBE, DSC, in command.

It was not quite the Malta of pre-war, but it still had some of its former splendour. There was still a Mediterranean Fleet, with a full Admiral, Sir Arthur John Power, as C-in-C. Rear Admiral Lord Louis Mountbatten was also there, commanding the 1st Cruiser Squadron. Mountbatten was always being accused of trying to 'manipulate' the Royal Family through his nephew, of trying to exert some powerful influence. 'Take Over' was a phrase often used. Such canards would have been much easier to refute (not that Lord Louis ever had any difficulty in persuading himself to ignore them) if his nephew had been appointed to a destroyer on some other Station.

But, Malta it was, and the Duke enjoyed it. The Princess came out to join her husband, like many another naval wife, although, unlike other naval wives, she flew out in a Viking of the King's Flight and was met at Luqa by the Governor, the Archbishop in his robes, the Prime Minister, and all the gold braid, red tabs and splendour of navy, army and air force high rank. The 'Edinburgh's', as some of the more cringe-making of the island's hostesses insisted on calling them, lived at the Villa Guardamangia at Pieta, which Lord Mountbatten had rented for £50 a month.

The house was modestly sized, but it had a very pleasant garden, with a walkway, and a good view over Marsascutto harbour. When *Chequers* was in dry dock, the Duke got up before seven o'clock every morning and drove down through the narrow streets to the dockyard at Sliema. For the Princess, it was a very enjoyable time, remarkably free from royal constraints. She had a detective trailing behind her, but she was able to go shopping, go to the hairdressers, have tea and lunch parties, watch the polo, swim and picnic.

It was, on the whole, a tranquil period, for once free of the 'Royal cage' of duty and engagements. All the same, royal duties were never far away. The Princess visited hospitals and schools, unveiled a war memorial, attended a rededication service in the Cathedral. *Chequers* sailed for the Red Sea shortly after Christmas and the Princess then went home. She was back in April, for her 24th birthday. The Duke had taken up polo and the Princess had more enjoyable afternoons watching her husband perform.

In July 1950, the Duke was promoted Lieutenant Commander, in the normal way after eight years seniority as a Lieutenant. That summer he took his Destroyer Command examination. For a 'salt-horse', i.e. non-specialist, officer, this was a vital hurdle to be crossed. All went well, except in the paper on torpedoes and sonar.

The C-in-C summoned Mike Parker, who was in Malta as the Duke's equerry, and showed him the paper saying, 'Who *is* this bloody examiner? He's failed him!' Arthur John Power said he had read the paper himself and thought it a 'damned good pass'. Although it seems highly unlikely for a man like Arthur John, apparently he let Mike Parker go away with the definite impression that he was going to 'put it right'.

To the Duke, the idea of being given something just because of his position was intolerable. Quite possibly, he also resented the implication that he did not have the right to fail occasionally, just like anybody else. He also had the awful suspicion that 'they' were about to 'arrange it' so that he passed anyway. 'If they try and fix it, I leave the Navy for good,' he said. So he sat the paper again, and passed.

Malta life went on; the Governor gave a Ball for the Royal couple. The Duke played polo for Mountbatten's team, the 'Shrimps', at the Marsa Club. He sailed his Flying Fifteen *Coweslip* in Sliema Harbour. The 'Edinburgh's' helped with the swings and slides at a children's party.

Having passed his exam, the Duke got his command, the frigate *Magpie*, in the 2nd Frigate Squadron, also in Malta. He joined her early in September 1950 and told her six officers and 186 men he meant to make her one of the finest ships in the Navy. They soon found out that 'Dukey' meant what he said. Some of them remember his command with pleasure. Others say he 'stamped about like a f—ing tiger'. It seems that the Duke had the Mountbatten determination to do well, with not quite the old Mountbatten magic over men's hearts.

The Duke was in an extraordinary position. He was the junior captain in the Squadron and *Magpie* was therefore the 'canteen boat'. But ashore, the Duke was senior even to the C-in-C himself. There were other problems, not obvious to the sailors who grumbled about the *Magpie* being 'Daddy's f—ing yacht'.

The husband of the heir to the throne, commanding his own warship, was too good a political and diplomatic card for the government not to play. The Duke and *Magpie* went hither and thither, carrying out their own individual brand of 'gunboat diplomacy'. In November the Duke represented the King at the opening of the new Legislative Council in Gibraltar. He called on King Ibn Saud of Saudi Arabia, and King Abdullah of Jordan, visited the President of Turkey, went to Cyprus and Egypt and Algeria.

The Duke was given no special facilities. He had to deal with his Royal correspondence while still running his ship as captain. He literally wrote out signals on one side of the forms and his royal speeches (which took him hours to compose) on the other. When the King of Greece went on board *Magpie* in Athens he was amazed to see that the Duke had no extra secretarial or communications staff. Mike Parker was equerry, but he was ashore; there was no room for him on board. Far from getting sympathy, the Duke had to endure scarcely concealed whispers about 'Edinburgh's private yacht'!

The C-in-C had lent his Despatch vessel *Surprise* for the trip to Athens. The Princess was on board, with *Magpie* as part of the escort. For a Duke it was a glad, but somewhat sad, visit. It was the first time he had been able to show his wife his own land. But so much had happened since his family had been forced to leave it.

The Duke flew home to attend the opening of the Festival of Britain in May 1951. On 16th July he gave up his command. He was given a 'royal salute' of 21 smoke floats. His officers rowed him ashore in the whaler. It was, and he must have known it at the time, the end of his active sea-going career.

Royal duties now closed around him. The King was a very sick man. His daughter, and her husband, had to take his place more often. In the autumn the King had an operation to remove his left lung. The Duke and the Princess undertook the tour of Canada which the King would have made.

On 31st January 1952 they left for a tour of Australia and New Zealand, flying first to Kenya. The King saw them off at London airport. On 6th February, the King died in his sleep. It was Mike Parker who had to break the news to the Duke. 'I never felt so sorry for anyone in all my life,' he said. 'He looked as though you'd dropped half the world in him.'

The Duke was promoted Commander in July 1952, and Admiral of the Fleet (as well as Field Marshal and Marshal of the Royal Air Force) in January 1953.

In the Duke's own opinion, as expressed to the cadets in *Devonshire* at their prize-giving only a few months later, he had served 'about half a Dog Watch' in the Navy. But he had three points he wanted to make, three fallacies about the Navy he wished to expose. In a way, they expressed his own philosophy, if that is not too pompous a word.

'First of all there is no such thing as a career for a naval officer. Service in the Navy is a privilege enjoyed by those who prove themselves capable of discharging the duties imposed upon them satisfactorily. Promotion is not a question of 'jobs for the boys'; it is a competition of service in the interest of the Navy and the country… If you put the interest of the Royal Navy first at all times, you will be acting in the best tradition of the Sea Service.'

'Second is the fallacy that a good seaman is necessarily a good naval officer. There is absolutely no doubt whatever that every naval officer must have a full and comprehensive sea-going experience. But the best interests of the Service demands a great deal more than that. Why is it that experienced people are chosen for responsible jobs? It is because in making decisions they are able to draw upon their experience which will prevent their making mistakes.

'It follows, therefore, that the foundation of a naval officer's experience must be his seamanship, but the wider his knowledge, and the broader his outlook, the more easily and ably he will shoulder responsibilities. His outlook must encompass the function and importance of the men and ships of the Navy, the relationship of the Services to one another and the State, and their responsibilities in defence of the realm.'

'The third fallacy I put forward with trepidation. It is contained in the famous preamble to the Naval Discipline Act and reads: "… relating to the Government of the Navy whereon under the good providence of God, the wealth, safety and strength of the Kingdom *chiefly* depends…" That was certainly true at the time it was written. The safety and strength of this country, Commonwealth and Empire now can only be ensured by power at sea, on land, and in the air. In the event of war, the enemy can only be defeated by action at sea, on land, and in the air...

'... In conclusion, I wish you all who are standing here at the beginning of your life in the Navy the greatest happiness and success in the Naval Service.'

HRH THE PRINCE OF WALES

Unlike his father, his grandfather and his great-grandfather, the Prince of Wales knew when he joined the Navy that he was not going to make his permanent career in the Service. There seems to have been some agreement in the Royal Family that the Prince should spend some time in the Services, as though it were part of his general higher education. He had already served in the RAF, and won his wings with them in August 1971.

He certainly would not have thought of taking a permanent commission in the Navy, even if it had been possible. 'I don't think I was ideally suited for the Navy', he says himself. 'Besides, it would have been selfish to have locked oneself away in one Service'. There would always be many other claims on his time. 'I would have been called away more and more, to do things.' The Prince has very close personal and family links with the Army. 'I'm colonel of six regiments, some of them have two battalions. I like to get round and visit them all at least once a year.'

There was an element of careful prior arrangement about his naval service. 'My whole programme,' he says, 'was mapped out before I joined.' The Prince went to Dartmouth, like his father and grandfather, in September 1971. Despite his RAF wings, his university degree, and his Royal family, the *Britannia* Royal Naval College received Acting Sub-Lieutenant HRH The Prince of Wales, as it receives all newcomers, without visible emotion. There was a great deal of drilling, with and without rifles, and doubling around the place, and boat-handling, and a swimming test, and exercises in the gym, and lectures on seamanship and radar and navigation.

Of his Dartmouth days, and all the hurrying and scurrying, the Prince now says that 'it was exactly like going back to prep school, after being at university.' Although he enjoyed his University time immensely, the Prince is still not absolutely convinced of its total relevance to life in the Services. He feels the Services, and particularly the RAF, were far too impressed with university graduates. 'The services went overboard with excitement about having graduates. I think they were *over-excited*.'

On training generally, the Prince believes 'we should all serve a minimum of six months in the ranks — on the lower deck. You can't motivate people without yourself having done what they have done. You must be able to think, how was *I* treated myself when I was in their position?'

The Prince of Wales seems always conscious of time pressing on him. Because of his position, he simply is never allowed the same time as everybody else. As a natural pilot, with his father's physical co-ordination of hand and eye and foot, he was able to complete the RAF flying course, normally a year, in five months. He was only at Dartmouth for six weeks, but he went about his course with awesome zeal, taking books and lecture notes ashore with him and studying them when he might have been relaxing. He had his reward in the results. As his great-uncle Lord Mountbatten said, 'My nephew was top in navigation and top in seamanship, and that is all we seamen care about.'

Nevertheless, the Prince is conscious of deficiencies. 'I would have been more competent if I'd stayed longer,' he says. 'There is no substitute for professional training.' He calls himself, faintly ironically, the 'last of the gentlemen amateurs' but the word 'professional' crops up in his conversation again and again. He is what is known as an 'achiever' and officers who served with him noticed that it was not enough for him to do as others did. He always wanted to land his helicopter, bring his ship alongside, just that little more smoothly and accurately than anybody else. He did not always achieve it. But it was not for want of trying.

The Prince's grandfather might have been at Jutland, his father at Matapan, but they were not heirs to the throne at the time, and the Prince always knew that the same service, or anything even remotely controversial, was never to be allowed to him. His private detective might be left on shore when he embarked in one of H.M. Ships, but he was still aware of the extra effort, the personnel, maintenance, fire-fighting, and communications, which his presence demands on board.

The choice of ship the Prince could serve in was severely limited by political cautions. He could not serve in a Polaris submarine — their purpose was, after all, avowedly and openly anti-Soviet. He could not serve in other submarines, in spite of his family's long history of alarms and excursions in the craft, because there simply was not time to undergo the course, although he did do the submarine escape training course in the 100-foot water tower at Gosport. Similarly, he could not serve in a frigate engaged in the Cod war against Icelandic gunboats, nor one taking part in the Beira Patrol, in the early days of sanctions against Rhodesia. When he took command of a minehunter, the vessel could not be employed, as others occasionally were, on the 'GRANADA' anti-gun-running patrols off the Irish coast.

The Prince's first ship, the County Class guided missile destroyer HMS *Norfolk*, seemed an innocuous choice. But the way in which his presence on board could easily be exploited was shown as soon as he joined. He flew out to join her at Gibraltar on Guy Fawkes' Day 1971, and at once the politically generated fireworks began. A stiff diplomatic Note from Madrid expressed official 'displeasure' at the presence of the Prince on 'Spanish territory' (actually it had not been Spanish for some two and a half centuries). The Note suggested that HRH's 'presence' in some unexplained way led to the 'revival of the dispute' and caused 'uncalled for injury to national sentiment, stirring up Spanish public opinion.' However, the Foreign Office advised that 'It is understood that the British Embassy merely considers it an informal advisory protest and not a diplomatic one.'

Gibraltar's Chief Minister, Major Robert Peliza, wrote to *The Times* that 'Whitehall has apparently gone to considerable lengths to avoid upsetting the Spanish Government when Prince Charles arrives...' For instance, he said, the Prince had been met by the Governor, Admiral Sir Varyl Begg, and not by the Chief Minister. Major Peliza said that had his electorate been consulted they would have 'strongly suggested giving the people of Gibraltar, in their eight years' siege, an opportunity to express publicly to Prince Charles their admiration and respect for the British Crown'. The Major said he himself would have thought it a 'profound honour' to welcome the Prince.

All this because a sub-lieutenant had joined his ship for training. But the episode demonstrates that no matter how hard the Prince of Wales tried to immerse himself in his naval career, external and political factors would always break in. The affair rumbled on for some little time. A planned visit by *Norfolk* to Malta was cancelled, although relations were later restored.

Some time later, when his ship was at 36 hours' notice to sail to Cyprus to render assistance to British nationals during one of the periodic conflagrations between Greek and Turkish Cypriots, the Prince discovered that if the ship had sailed he would have been flown ashore to Malta en route 'for some job on the staff, or something equally fatuous'. Once again, he could not be allowed into a controversial situation. He would have missed the excitement, and as it occurred to him, missed the chance of a possible medal. He has the family Mountbatten's affinity for medals. 'I would have *loved* to have got a medal,' he says. He actually has two: the 1953 Coronation Medal, and the 1977 Jubilee Medal but he evidently discounts those, as naval officers have always tended to do, as 'Mickey Mouse' medals, not to be compared with 'proper' campaign medals.

In *Norfolk*, the Prince followed the same routine as any other officer under training. He kept a log of his activities, wrote up descriptions of the ship's machinery, armament and electronic equipment, traced pipework, kept watches, on the bridge and below, took charge of the sea-boat when it was called away. He was still very conscious of his ignorance. 'I suspect that people thought I knew more about it than I did. Having a stripe on your arm means that you know it, when you really don't. When a sailor looks at a gold stripe he thinks you know what you're doing.'

The Prince spent Christmas at Windsor, and in the New Year underwent the submarine escape training course at HMS *Dolphin*, in Gosport. The course culminated in an ascent from a specially constructed 'submarine', fitted with escape hatch, breathing apparatus, and flooding valves, at the bottom of the 100-foot tank. On leaving the 'submarine', the escaper allows his inflated lifejacket to carry him rapidly to the surface. But the air in his lungs, inhaled at 100-foot pressure, necessarily expands on the way up. Thus the escaper must expel air from his lungs, breathing *out*, as he ascends — which seems against all nature. Under his self-imposed policy of asking no favours, cutting no corners, going the whole hog, the Prince completed the whole course. (The tank had a clean record for many years but training was temporarily suspended after two deaths — one the Deputy Command Escape Training Officer himself.)

Back in *Norfolk*, when the ship paid a visit to Toulon, the Prince went on a run ashore. It was a memorable evening, and an unforgettable morning after. 'We went to several bars, where I mixed my drinks, which I had never done before. I learned my lesson the hard way, by the way I felt afterwards. I never did that again.'

Later, as a helicopter pilot, the Prince was notable for his abstemiousness, in circles not noted for their teetotalism. They said of him in the carrier *Hermes* that 'he never got drunk, absolutely never, and he was a very good example to some of the younger pilots. He taught them that they didn't *have* to get smashed out of their tiny minds every night they weren't flying.' As the Prince himself says now, 'I've never seen the point of getting smashed out of your mind.'

The Prince's travels must have reassured many a likely lad, thinking of joining, that one could still join the Navy and see the world. As assistant gunnery officer of the frigate *Minerva*, which he joined in November 1972, he went to the West Indies. As communications officer *of Jupiter*, which he joined in January 1974, he went to Australia, New Zealand, Suva, Samoa, Fiji and California.

He lived the same strange double life. At sea and on board, he was a junior officer, with his own way to make, with much to learn and not much time to learn it in. Once ashore, he was transmogrified into the Prince of Wales, and exchanged courtesy visits with local dignitaries, attended openings of Parliaments and ceremonies of independence, hobbed and nobbed with celebrities, the centre of a circle of intense scrutiny at receptions, dances, parades and parties.

There were still scares. An officer with a history of mental disturbance broke into the Prince's cabin one night in *Osprey* at Portland. When *Minerva* visited Bermuda, the Prince had dinner with the Governor Sir Richard Sharpies. A week later, the Governor and an aide Captain Hugh Sayers were shot and killed whilst walking round the Residency garden one evening after dinner. There was a strong suspicion that the assassin thought Sayers was the Prince of Wales. Thus, when *Minerva* next visited Bermuda, there was no question of the Prince still being on board. He transferred to the hydrographic survey ship HMS *Fox* at Antigua.

His fellow officers came to know the Prince well, but, as they said themselves, they learned from observation, not from confidences, and they learned nothing at all from him about other members of the family. He was, as they all say, a 'brilliant listener', genuinely interested in people. But he kept his own counsel, and was an expert at holding people at arm's length, fending off or laughing off any real enquiry.

The Prince has, very well developed, his family's talent for appearing free and informal whilst really giving nothing away. He always maintained a careful line between acquaintance and familiarity. In *Jupiter* there was an incident of almost symbolic significance. The wardroom officers tried to 'debag' the Prince, but he successfully fought off the would-be debaggers. Evidently there was a firm line between what he would permit and what he was determined to resist.

This iron self-discipline, which is not an imposed mask, but much more a way of life, would have ordinary mortals screaming with frustration inside a year. Never to drop one's guard, never to vouchsafe confidences, even late at night and in one's cups, never to be rude or give offence even unconsciously, never to offer the slightest hostage to gossip or scandal, demands an almost unimaginable effort of self-control. It must run in the family, and in fact there are remarkable resemblances between the pressures, incidents, and itineraries of some of the Prince of Wales' tours and those of his great-uncle the Prince of Wales, who became Edward VIII.

The last Prince of Wales used to avoid handshakes, and he took an old courtier's advice, to relieve himself whenever he could. The present Prince, while heeding the same advice, also feels that 'the most important thing is to learn when to laugh. I have a motto, when in doubt, laugh.'

For a selfish personality, a lifestyle such as the Prince's would be intolerable. The only way such pressures can be withstood is by a genuine, self-renewing, concern for other people which normally brings with it the ability to see the right action and the right moment to take it. When *Jupiter* was in Brisbane, one of the Prince's signals staff, Neil Race, was killed in a motor accident. His belongings were later auctioned — a custom dating back to the days of sail — with the proceeds going to his next-of-kin. The bidding raised the remarkable sum of £1,500, the Prince himself setting the pace, bidding £60 for a pair of socks, £100 for a suitcase, and then (as was often done on the messdeck) putting them up for auction again.

In October 1974 the Prince went to the Royal Naval Air Station, Yeovilton, in Somerset, to accomplish one of his heart's desires, to learn to fly a naval helicopter. As he says, 'I was absolutely thrilled to be flying in the Navy. I shall never forget the thrill of it.' He would also have liked to fly Buccaneers and Phantoms, but that was forbidden.

A special flight, with some 20 maintenance ratings, called Red Dragon Flight, was formed to 'fly the Prince'. But once again, time's winged chariot was hurrying near. The Prince spent 45 days at Yeovilton, spread over some three months because his training was constantly being interrupted; often the Prince would carry out a full day's training down in Somerset and fly to London in the evening to carry out an engagement.

In spite of all the many calls on his time, the Prince completed 105 flying hours, 26 of them solo, in his Wessex V helicopter, call-sign Whisky Alpha. On his first solo day, the Prince's instructor, Lieutenant Commander Alan MacGregor said before climbing out, 'OK, you're on your own now, so I'm going back to the tower.' The Prince replied, 'If I crash this heap, that's where you're going to spend the rest of your life!'

The Prince passed out as a fully-qualified pilot on 12th December 1974, having won the Double Diamond award as the trainee pilot who made the most progress. There had been dramas and successes. He had been forced to make at least three emergency landings ('precautionary landings' as the Palace press releases called them) for engine or component failures. He sometimes had difficulty in totting up his flying hours in his Aircraft Servicing Log, (so as to get cumulative totals on which maintenance routines were carried out).

On the rocket firing range at Castlemartin in Pembrokeshire he showed himself a natural pilot. The course included not only his own instructor but several fellow trainees, future squadron COs, and helicopter warfare instructors. He was the only pilot that week to score a direct rocket hit on the target. Red Dragon Flight got the customary bottle of champagne.

The Prince's passing-out day happened also to be the tenth anniversary of No. 707 training squadron's formation. There was a fly-past to celebrate. Each helicopter in turn flew past the air traffic control tower, the Prince streaming his personal standard on the winch-wire.

The Prince had a considerable gift for repartee, which may not translate well on to the printed page, but at the time, in the circumstances, and sometimes delivered in his 'Neddie Seagoon' voice, had the sailors in stitches. Walking round Whisky Alpha before night-flying, he asked for a torch, switched it on and had an eyeful of white light. A goon voice said, 'There's my night vision gone for a burton!'

Early in 1975 the Prince achieved another of his great ambitions, to fly in an operational squadron from an operational aircraft carrier. He attributes his luck to Commander Rob Woodard, then CO of 848 Squadron. 'He said, You ought to come with us, we're going to *Bulwark*. Well, I didn't go to *Bulwark* but I did go to *Hermes*, and I'm deeply indebted to him.'

The Squadron eventually chosen was 845, embarked in *Hermes*. Chief Aircraft Artificer Abnett took half Red Dragon Flight down to Plymouth a day early, to meet the aircraft and the Prince the next day. When the Prince arrived, Chief Abnett said 'he seemed visibly relieved to see us and this reinforced my view that he liked people around him whom he knew. Particularly amongst strangers. During his period in the Fleet Air Arm there were numerous people who tried to become hangers-on and better their careers. Once, when HRH was walking out to his aircraft a Lieutenant Commander who had obviously been waiting his chance rushed out from a side building and got in step with him. A few words were exchanged and the Lieutenant Commander slunk off with his tail between his legs after receiving a rebuke. It is my impression that the Prince only liked and related to genuine people.'

The Prince spent his time in 845 metaphorically holding his breath, as though not quite believing it was happening. 'I used to say to myself, this can't be', he says. 'Something is going to happen to stop it. But it didn't.' The wistful pleasure in his voice shows that this was one of the happiest, most fulfilling, most liberated times of his life.

Flying aircraft from carriers at sea does have hazards. The Prince accepted them, and enjoyed them, although it was obvious, as always, that special arrangements were made for him: the extra effort in maintenance and spares to achieve as near perfect reliability as possible, the second helicopter, with back-up crew, the fire-fighting gear, and the added watchfulness on the flightdeck, with tension screwed up a further notch.

The Prince had divisional duties and was very popular with the sailors as defending counsel up at the Commander's defaulters' table, no matter how hopeless the case. The defendants wanted to be able to tell their grandchildren, 'I had the King of England defending me and I *still* didn't get off!'

Hermes' deployment took her to the West Indies and to Fort Lauderdale in Florida, where the Prince had to fly home for royal engagements, leaving Red Dragon Flight to hold the fort in his absence, showing American visitors where 'the Prince keeps his polo ponies in the hangar' and reassuring them that 'yes, he certainly does eat his meals with his crown on.'

In Montreal, the Prince was back in time for a huge cocktail party in that same hangar. The Commander decided that HRH probably needed protection from the local talent. 'We'll have to look after you, with all these young things about.'

'Oh no,' said HRH, 'it's not the daughters, it's the *mothers* who come up and pinch me on the backside.'

'Sure enough, when the cocktail party was in full swing, suddenly before anybody could stop her, some blue-rinsed veteran came right up behind HRH and *perclunk!* she grabbed a double handful.'

'He didn't bat an eyelid. He just looked round and said, 'What did I tell you?'

One of the main reasons for *Hermes'* deployment was a large scale Commando assault exercise, lasting for some six weeks, in the Canadian forests around Fredericton, New Brunswick. 845 Squadron and Red Dragon Flight flew ashore to an old, disused airfield, inappropriately called Blissville.

The weather at Blissville soon turned horrid, and somebody had forgotten to bring the rations; two hundred or so aircrew, with twenty aircraft, miles from civilisation, had no solid food for two days. When the stores did arrive, the cooking was done by the stewards who as Chief Abnett said, 'could even ruin boiling water.' At last, the Prince sent his private detective into Fredericton to find a restaurant, booked tables for thirty, and took the whole Flight out to their first decent meal for weeks.

Despite the cold, the appalling weather and food, the Prince kept his gift for repartee. He grew a beard and seemed nonplussed when the sailors asked him what the Queen would think about it. He thought for a space and then said, 'I know what I'll do — I'll shave one half off and walk in sideways when I get home.'

After *Hermes*, the Prince did command courses and in February 1976, faced his biggest naval test, command of his own ship. He joined her at Rosyth on 9th February. She was HMS *Bronington*, named after a small Flintshire village, on the Welsh borders. She was 360 tons, had a length of 159 feet, a top speed of 15 knots, and a complement of five officers and 34 sailors. Her job was minehunting, for which she had a wooden hull with aluminium fittings (so as not to activate magnetic mines), very accurate sonar sets, so-called 'active rudders' with small propellors in their trailing edges to give extra manoeuvrability, and specially trained clearance divers.

With her high bluff bows, chunky, functional look and upper deck cluttered with booms, sweeps and gear, *Bronington* was no oil painting. She rolled prodigiously in quite innocuous seas, and at 23 years old, she was no spring chicken either. But she was the Prince's first command and, like every other young man in his position, he thought she was fairer than any dream of women.

She was in the First Mine Counter-measures Squadron, with Commander D. C. W. Elliott as Senior Officer. Also in the squadron were the Exercise Minelayer *Abdiel*, and two other *Ton* Class, *Maxton* and *Bildeston*. The Prince was not quite the most junior captain (*Bildeston*'s C.O. was actually junior to him) so *Bronington* was not the 'canteen boat'.

But the Prince did not need anybody to tell him that, as his father would have said, he had only been in the Navy less than half a dog-watch. His service had been constantly interrupted. He did not have the same breadth of naval experience as the other COs. It says a great deal for the Prince's application and quickness to learn that the Admiralty ever seriously considered him at all for an independent command.

His first signal was from Flag Officer, Royal Yachts, Rear Admiral H. P. Janion:

> The Royal Yachtsmen old and new
> Humbly send these words to you:
> May fair winds and good fortune be
> Forever in your company.

But what about, oh captain new,
A Ton class painted royal blue?

To which *Bronington* replied:

My gratitude is more than due
To all those Yachties old and new
For such a message of good cheer
Which I shall always hold most dear.
Perhaps I should just mention here
That if we meet at sea this year
Be sure to keep your fenders out
Lest your paint gets spread about.

Fenders were required on *Bronington*'s first trip to sea under the new management. The Prince had had very little chance to practise his ship-handling and his first day could not have been more testing. It was a raw February Rosyth afternoon, with a Force 6 gusting to Force 7 wind from the North Sea blowing over the quarter (old Rosyth hands will recognise the description). With two shafts and 'active rudders', the *Ton* Class are very manoeuvrable, but their high freeboard makes them liable to gather leeway in any wind, and there was some understandable tension, and some mildly chewed lips, on the upper-deck and on the jetty as *Bronington* approached.

But all went well. As the First Lieutenant Roy Clare said, the Prince 'was a model ship-handler. He didn't lose any dignity at all over it. It was a quite horrific day for your first alongside, but it was no problem in the end.'

The officers and ship's company (all of whom were very young: the sailors had an average age of 19½; Clare, the oldest officer, was 25) soon found out that the Prince had been extensively briefed beforehand, to cover every eventuality. But they also discovered that the brief seemed to hark back to much larger ships and to an age that was past, a Navy of rum and hammocks and furnace fuel oil. The brief (it was not hard to guess at the identity of its 'onlie begetter') covered such things as 'airing the ship's company bedding'. In fact, everybody slept in sleeping bags.

However, slowly, the Prince relaxed and began to put away his notes when 'he found out that the water was not actually coming in through the side — not yet, anyway.'

Another problem, which had never troubled the Prince of Wales before, was seasickness. The *Ton* Class were lively movers in any seaway and *Bronington*'s particular harmonic motion clashed violently with the Prince's personal rhythms. He fought it grimly, as though seasickness was a reflection on his manhood, a failure in male macho, and not an inescapable physical condition, like vertigo or short-sightedness.

The others used to watch the Prince 'getting himself into a state about it, absolutely determined not to give way, it was quite painful to watch him, but then, when it got rough enough, over he went.'

His great struggle against seasickness was only one manifestation of the Prince's determination to ask no favours, have no concessions, no allowances made, but to be treated in every way and every day exactly like everybody else. To him, as to his father, the thought of any deference to his rank was anathema. 'I would have left the Navy the very next day,' he said, 'if I'd ever had to say to anybody, you must do this because I am telling you and I am the Prince of Wales. I never once had to do that, and I would have resigned at once if I ever had.'

Alone, he wrestled with *Bronington*'s officers' heads. The Prince's interest in matters lavatorial runs like a leit-motif (loo-motif, perhaps) through his service. He once persuaded a hotel-keeper in Barry, South Wales, to present him with a splendid collectors' item of a Victorian loo. In *Bronington*, he met his match. The flushing arrangements, if not handled with the utmost delicacy, reacted violently and sprayed the whole compartment. They seemed to recognise 'his master's touch' and reserved their most spectacular water-effects for the Prince's presence.

With his great talent for being a good listener and his intense interest in people, the Prince of Wales thought deeply about the motivations of the men under his command. Talking today of his naval career, in his private sitting-room in Buckingham Palace, it is this problem of the individual which seems most central to his experience in the Navy. 'You must know about other people's motivations, and think about their welfare and morale,' he says. 'The most important thing in all this is the morale of the individual. You must pay attention to that. People will work far harder and much better if they can see the *point* of doing things.'

Certainly, some of *Bronington*'s sailors gave the Prince plenty of raw material for study (the ship's company were not 'selected' for their 'suitability' in any way and included as many 'skates' and malefactors as any other small ship). As the Prince says, 'there were several difficult Glaswegians and Geordies on board who would have made life utterly impossible if not handled properly'.

Because of his position, there were bound to be vast areas of his sailors' lives which were strange to the Prince (of *Bronington*'s food he said, when he first arrived, 'this is rather like camping, isn't it?'). As Captain, he had to deal with the ship's money matters. Like every member of the Royal Family, he was not used to handling actual money, and it was only half-jokingly that the other officers produced for him a spoof card, illustrating the coins of the realm and their values.

But it was in domestic matters that most surrealist moments occurred, as the Prince grappled with the realities of life in the poorer parts of Glasgow. There was, as they still say on board, one sailor, a Glaswegian, who was always late back from his leave, and with a different excuse every time. One morning, he explained that his wife had recently bought a budgerigar. During the night, the budgie escaped, flew round the bedroom and eventually jumped on the alarm clock, turning off the bell. Hence it did not ring, hence the sailor was late on board. 'The Prince just listened to all this in stupefaction, then roared with laughter and dismissed the case.'

In *Bronington*, the Prince was taken away for royal duties much less than before, but still, every three days, a large blue dispatch bag would arrive on board and the Prince had to spend long hours on official correspondence. There was also a huge unofficial correspondence, of requests for cap ribbons, for interviews and autographs, all of which were declined as politely as possible.

The Prince read all the newspapers every day he could. The press generally maintained a close watch on the ship. The Prince recognised that this interest was part of his job. 'There would be something wrong, if they weren't interested,' he said. 'It would mean I wasn't doing my job properly.' Nevertheless, the other officers would see him, in the wardroom, or through the door of his little cabin, reading the papers and 'frowning and scowling at something they had said about his sister'.

The ship's company took the keenest interest in the ladies the Prince invited on board. Most of the girls were taken aback by the 'pokiness' of the wardroom and the CO's cabin. One suggested the ship should have more cushions and actually provided some, but they soon disappeared as souvenirs. The Prince went to sea for a day in *Bronington* in February 1981 (he talks somewhat nostalgically of having a proper reunion someday). It was the day before the news of his engagement was released to the world's press; in his own words, the day before the storm breaks'. *Bronington* was given the news beforehand, but not a man on board broke the secret.

The sailors seemed unsurprised by the Prince's engagement The general opinion was that 'There was no way he was going to be King without having himself a Queen, was there? He was bound to pick one or other of them sooner or later.'

Bronington joined in the squadron activities and visits that spring and summer of 1976. There was a 12-day NATO exercise CENTEX, in the Irish Sea. with the Standing Naval Force Channel and three Royal Naval Reserve vessels; squadron exercises in the Channel; a visit to Workington, a three-day squadron visit to Dartmouth, and a four-day visit with *Bildeston* to Barry. The Prince grew another beard. His great-uncle, the Admiral of the Fleet, came for a day at sea.

At Torbay, the squadron received a distress call; a diver was missing in 165 feet of water off Bolt Head. The squadron swept for five hours but found nothing. *Bronington* was sent at short notice to shadow a Russian 'Whisky' Class submarine passing through the Straits of Dover. For all these episodes, the Prince's detective stayed ashore, driving the Royal Range Rover from place to place, picking up the ship's milk and mail and, as the sailors said, 'Making himself quite useful — for a copper.'

In November *Bronington* visited the Pool of London and spent her Captain's 28th birthday alongside a pier close to the Tower (at last, the subject of so many jokes and threats during the Prince's naval career). The Captain's family came on board to look over his ship. A splendid page in the ship's visitors' book records their signatures: H.M. the Queen, the Duke of Edinburgh, the Queen Mother, Princess Anne, Captain Mark Phillips, Prince Edward, Princess Alice, Duchess of Gloucester, the Duke and Duchess of Gloucester, Princess Alexandra and Mr Angus Ogilvy. They met the officers and the ship's company, squeezed into the smallest compartments, exclaimed at the 'tiddly' appearance of the upper deck, complimented the design of the special ship's badge, in fact behaved like any other family coming to see their son/grandson/nephew/brother/cousin's ship.

The Prince's final ceremony on board was Christmas dinner. Following another ancient naval custom, the Prince as Captain waited at table, while his Royal 'woolly pully' was worn by his Leading Steward Ron Patterson, who had served with the Prince almost throughout his naval service.

Of all the members of his family who have served in the Navy, the Prince of Wales probably established the closest *rapport* with the lower deck. The sailors recognised a trier when they saw one. They enjoyed his company. They liked to serve with him, as a man and an officer, quite apart from his royal connections. It is a noticeable common factor of all reminiscences of the Prince of Wales: how much those who served with him enjoyed the experience and looked back on those days with the greatest pleasure.

It was not likely that *Bronington* would let the Prince go without some sort of ceremony. He had once rashly remarked that 'Command has aged me' and on the morning of 14th December a wheelchair duly arrived alongside. The royal carriage was further distinguished by the Order of the Throne, a brilliantly polished lavatory seat garlanded with a roll of toilet paper. The Prince was wheeled away in state, to tremendous cheers from *Bronington* and other ships in company.

The Prince's final act was a 'command performance' variety show ashore in Rosyth, attended by the ship's company and their families. Harry Secombe was the top of the bill, he and other artistes giving their services for nothing. Some £120 was raised for the RN & RM Children's Home at Waterlooville, Hants.

The Prince of Wales was promoted Commander the next day, and his active naval service came to an end. As one of *Bronington*'s sailors said, 'It's going to seem a bit dull after all this.'

As for that 'Order of the Throne' send-off, it was widely reported in the press, with pictures and quotes (Prince: 'See you behave yourself, lads'; Leading Medical Assistant 'Doc' Kevin Ryan: 'See you keep your bowels open, sir'). There was an unexpected and unpleasant sequel. Five days later, a letter appeared in the *Daily Telegraph*: 'Sir: As an old time naval officer who has served 44 years in the Royal Navy, I have never seen a more disgraceful event than the send-off from the Royal Navy of our Queen's son (Dec. 16).

'No doubt HRH's great good humour enabled him to accept this, but can anyone think he enjoyed it?

'Surely there should have been some petty officer or officer to give a better guidance to a very young crew.

'Having had the honour of being commanded by the Prince of Wales, one could have thought the ship's company would have been able to fix up something appropriate for one actually leaving a great Service.' The letter was signed H. T. Baillie-Grohman (a retired admiral, living near Chichester) who also sent another letter, in even stronger terms, to the ship.

Lieutenant Roy Clare, who organised the send-off, was unrepentant. 'We didn't give him a row-ashore-in-the-Captain's-gig sort of send-off because he simply is not a row-ashore-in-the-Captain's-gig sort of guy. It was a measure of what the Navy thought of him that they were prepared to go to that amount of trouble for him.'

To the admiral himself, Clare replied: 'I take full responsibility for the arrangements made for our farewell to the Prince: we were very sorry to see him leave and had all enjoyed a memorable year in the company of a man whom we respect deeply and to whom we all became devoted. Such was the charm and good humour of HRH, it seemed entirely natural that we should honour him with a practical joke after his own heart. This we tried to do and I am disappointed that you did not see the fun of the occasion. I can only hope to allay your fears that we may have offended the Prince by assuring you that he was delighted with our jape and seemed only to be disappointed that we had not carried him ashore on a Neil Robertson stretcher.

'Lieutenant the Prince of Wales is now, more simply, His Royal Highness and it is unthinkable that anyone should ever again be able to pull his leg in such a public manner: we have indeed been privileged and the Ship's Company — as stout a bunch as ever sailed in your flotillas — are well aware of their good fortune.'

Clare received support in the same columns from Mr William Bathurst, of Broadstairs, who thought 'the Prince of Wales's send-off from the Royal Navy, in retrospect at least, must have given him deep satisfaction' and from Captain S. Le H. Lombard-Hobson, RN, of Laughton, Sussex:

'Sir — I was wondering who would be the first old-time naval officer to write to you on the subject of the send-off accorded to the commanding officer of HMS *Bronington*. Vice Admiral H. T. Baillie-Grohman expresses exactly the same feeling that I had when I saw the picture of this "disgraceful" ceremony in the Press, and on television.

'I wonder, however, if the scene was really as dreadful as the Admiral describes it, remembering that the Prince of Wales was present in his capacity as a well-liked and very junior commanding officer and not as heir to the throne.'

After describing certain traditional leave-taking rites in the Navy, Captain Lombard-Hobson remembered 'when serving as a midshipman in the Mediterranean Fleet during the early 1930s, once reporting to the commander for night rounds in the wardroom where not only the then Prince of Wales, but his brother, both of whom were later to succeed to the throne of England, were being entertained to the usual wild guest-night dinner. The songs and the parlour tricks to which these two most distinguished royal guests were being subjected made the "humour" served on Prince Charles seem drawing room stuff in comparison.'

Finally, Captain Lombard-Hobson said. 'I well understand what Admiral Baillie-Grohman was getting at: I shared his feelings — initially. Perhaps we are both getting a bit stuffy!'

The whole episode of the 'Throne' and its aftermath was most revealing on naval attitudes towards the Royal Family, past and present. Significantly, the Prince of Wales invited Clare (who had in 1981, by a coincidence of naval appointing, become captain of *Bronington* himself) to be an usher in St Paul's Cathedral on the big day. The 1981 ship's company subscribed to an oil painting of *Bronington* as a wedding present.

It is difficult to imagine King George V being trundled along the jetty in a wheelchair when he left one of his commands. But the Prince of Wales lost no dignity over the affair, which in itself encapsulated in one short episode the way in which the relationship between the Royal Family and the Royal Navy has changed, and yet has remained exactly the same as it always was.

Certainly no present member of the Royal Family has anything like the direct influence on the Navy that King George V had. King George V was concerned with a great deal more in the Navy than the choice of warships' names. He was a powerful political figure and 'What does the King think?' was not just a formal petition addressed for the sake of protocol to the titular head of the Navy, but a question of real importance. A measure opposed by His Majesty might still be carried out. A personality disapproved of by His Majesty might still be appointed or promoted. But the First Lord, or the First Sea Lord, or whoever was responsible for the decision, would know by the end that a formidable obstacle had been surmounted.

Today, all that has changed. The Prince of Wales himself disclaims any influence at all. 'I don't have any influence on the Navy,' he says. 'I don't mind firing off a letter to somebody every now and again. It sometimes works. I never mind asking. As I always say, they can always say no.'

His influence was by no means as negligible as he claims. His mere presence in the Navy, as a serving officer, taking part in service affairs, appearing on service occasions, did the Navy immeasurable good. To put it at its crudest, it was splendid public relations for the Navy for people to see and read of him piloting his helicopter, bringing his ship alongside, making a parachute jump, surfacing in the 100-foot escape tank, wearing a shallow-water or deep diving suit.

Looking back now, the Prince says 'I learned a lot from the Navy. It did me the world of good. I've been in it, I like to think I put a certain amount of effort into the Navy, and I have a right to speak about it thereafter. I still take a great interest in it. I made a lot of friends in the Navy and I still keep up with them. Maybe when they get into more senior positions I shall have more say in things. I haven't much now. Times have changed.'

Once again, as one member leaves, another takes his place. Midshipman HRH Prince Andrew joined the *Britannia* Royal Naval College in September 1979 to undergo a course to become a helicopter pilot. Once again, those great sweeping stone corridors of Dartmouth echoed to the sound of Royal boots pounding on their way to lectures or divisions.

On present form, the new man is another achiever, following in father's and brother's footsteps. At Culdrose on 2nd April 1981, Admiral of the Fleet HRH Prince Philip, Duke of Edinburgh, KG, KT, OM, GBE, presented helicopter flying wings to Midshipman HRH The Prince Andrew CVO, and also the Louis Newmark Trophy for the best flying marks. Prince Andrew has gone on to train to fly Sea King helicopters in an operational squadron.

SOURCES & ACKNOWLEDGEMENTS

The extracts from *King George V*, by Harold Nicolson (Constable: London, 1952) and *King George VI*, by John W. Wheeler-Bennett (MacMillan: London, 1958) which are Royal copyright are published by the gracious permission of Her Majesty the Queen. The extracts from Prince Philip's Midshipman's Journal of 1940–41 are published by kind permission of His Royal Highness. The author and publisher would like to thank H.R.H. The Prince of Wales for granting a most informative and entertaining interview on his naval life and career at Buckingham Palace earlier this year at a time when, as it later transpired, he must have had many other more immediate matters, including matrimony, on his mind.

Abstracts of reports on King George V's naval career are in the Public Record Office: ADM. 196/20, p.489; ADM. 196/39, p.1382, and ADM. 196/42, p.255. Letters to Admiral Sir Henry F. Stephenson are from *A Royal Correspondence* (MacMillan: London, 1938), Ed. John Stephenson. Letters to and from Lord Fisher are from *Fear God and Dreadnought*, 3 vols., edited by Arthur J. Marder, (Cape: London, 1952–59). Acknowledgements and thanks are due to the authors and publishers of the above, and also to those of the following:

KING GEORGE V: Sir George Arthur, *King George V* (Cape: London, 1929); Admiral Sir Reginald Bacon, *Earl Jellicoe* (Cassell: London, 1936); Rear Admiral Gordon Campbell, VC, DSO, *Number Thirteen* (Hodder & Stoughton: London, 1932); Randolph S. Churchill, *Winston S. Churchill*, Vol. II, Young Statesman 1901–1914 (Heinemann: London, 1974); Admiral Sir Dudley de Chair, *The Sea is Strong* (Harrap: London, 1961);

John Gore, *King George V: A Personal Memoir* (John Murray: London, 1941); *Hail and Farewell: The Passing of King George V* (*The Times*: London, 1936); Admiral Mark Kerr, *Prince Louis of Battenberg* (Longmans, Green: London, 1934); Commander Stephen King-Hall, *A North Sea Diary 1914–1918* (Newnes: London); Commander Geoffrey L. Lowis, *Fabulous Admirals* (Putnam: London, 1957); Sir Owen Morshead, *George V* (D.N.B. 1931–1940: Oxford, 1949); Captain Stephen Roskill, *Naval Policy Between the Wars*, Vol.1 1919–1929, Vol.2 1930–1939 (Collins: London, 1968 and 1976); Lady Wester Wemyss, *Life & Letters of Lord Wemyss* (Eyre & Spottiswoode: London, 1935).

KING EDWARD VIII: *A Kings Story, The Memoirs of HRH the Duke of Windsor*, (Cassell: London, 1951); Frances Donaldson, *Edward VIII* (Weidenfeld & Nicholson: London, 1974); Major F. E. Verney, *H.R.H.* (Hodder & Stoughton: London, 1926).

KING GEORGE VI: Peter Cree, Midshipman's Journal, Home Fleet, 1943; Robert Hughes, *Through the Waters: HMS Scylla* (Kimber: London, 1956); Admiral Sir William James, *The Sky was Always Blue* (Methuen: London, 1951); Lieut. Cdr. P. K. Kemp, *Nine Vanguards* (Hutchinson: London, 1951); Commander Anthony Kimmins, *Half Time* (Heinemann: London, 1947); J.S.S.L., *Royal Naval Occasions*, (Naval Review: Vol.63, No.3, July 1975); James Moffatt, *King George Was My Shipmate*, (Stanley Paul: London, 1940); *The Silver Phantom: HMS Aurora*, by Her Company (Muller: London, 1945); Peter Townsend, *The Last Emperor* (Weidenfeld & Nicholson, 1975).

PRINCE PHILIP, DUKE OF EDINBURGH: Queen Alexandra of Yugoslavia, *Prince Philip: A Family Portrait* (Hodder & Stoughton: London, 1959); Commander David Bird; Basil Boothroyd, *Prince Philip: An Informal Biography*

(Longman: London, 1971), Admiral of the Fleet Viscount Cunningham, *A Sailor's Odyssey* (Hutchinson: London, 1951); Margit Fjellman, *Louise Mountbatten: Queen of Sweden* (Allen & Unwin: London, 1968); A. Cecil Hampshire, *Royal Sailors* (Kimber: London, 1971); Alden Hatch, *The Fabulous Mountbattens* (W. H. Allen: London, 1965); General Sir Leslie Hollis, *The Captain General* (Jenkins: London, 1961); Richard Hough, *Mountbatten: Hero of Our Time* (Weidenfeld & Nicholson: London, 1980); Michael Joyce; Denis Judd, *Prince Philip* (Michael Joseph: London, 1980); Peter Lane, *Prince Philip* (Robert Hale: London, 1980); W. A. Magill; *Newcastle Journal*; Eric Oates; Prince Philip, *Selected Speeches 1948–1955* (Oxford University Press, 1957); *Prince Philip Speaks*, Selected Speeches 1956–1959, (Collins: London, 1960); John Terraine, *The Life and Times of Lord Mountbatten* (Hutchinson: London, 1968).

THE PRINCE OF WALES: K. J. Abnett; Lieutenant R. A. G. Clare, AMNI, RN, the Officers and Ship's Company of *HMS Bronington*; Tim Heald and Mayo Mohs, *HRH: The Man Who Will Be King* (Sphere Books. London, 1979); Anthony Holden, *Charles Prince of Wales* (Weidenfeld & Nicholson: London, 1979).

A NOTE TO THE READER

If you have enjoyed this book enough to leave a review on **Amazon** and **Goodreads**, then we would be truly grateful.
The Estate of John Winton

Sapere Books is an exciting new publisher of brilliant fiction and popular history.

To find out more about our latest releases and our monthly bargain books visit our website: **saperebooks.com**

Printed in Great Britain
by Amazon

23178296R00086